The Complete Book of Spells

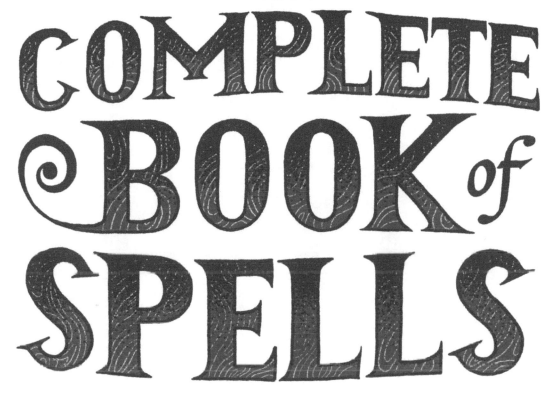

the COMPLETE BOOK of SPELLS

WICCAN SPELLS FOR HEALING, PROTECTION, AND CELEBRATION

DEBORAH·LIPP

Illustrations by Studio Muti

ROCKRIDGE
PRESS

Recipes for Maple Cookies (page 130) and White Sandwich Bread (page 164) provided courtesy of Heather Perine's *Beginner's Baking Bible*.

Interior and Cover Designer: Erik Jacobsen
Art Producer: Samantha Ulban
Editor: Jesse Aylen
Production Editor: Mia Moran
Illustrations © 2020 Studio Muti
Author photo courtesy of Marshall Reyher

ISBN: Print 978-1-64611-944-8 | eBook 978-1-64611-945-5
R0

To the Goddess living just outside
my window, Lady Liberty.

"I lift my lamp beside the golden door."
—Emma Lazarus

Contents

Introduction

TAKING YOUR FIRST STEPS INTO WICCA IS A JOY. Continuing those steps is a lifetime's journey.

I have been Wiccan since 1981 but felt a connection to nature long before. As a teenager, I was out in nature whenever possible, hearing Her voice, feeling Her call, and surrounded by Her. I knew that somewhere, somehow, I would worship the Goddess of Nature, and *all* the Old Gods, as my heart longed to do.

While it didn't strictly relate to my love of the Gods, I learned another powerful thing as a teen: I had the ability to do magic. Quite unintentionally, I found I could raise energy from my body. I was absolutely sure (and I turned out to be right!) that this was a power I could use, if I learned how.

Since then, I've dedicated myself to my practice, written seven other books on Wicca-related topics, trained dozens of people in magic and spellcasting, initiated many witches, made mistakes, learned from them, and never wavered from the path that has shaped my life. It's my hope that you, too, can find fulfillment, challenge, and growth on this path.

Spells and rituals aren't all there is to Wicca, but they're an important component. In these pages, you'll find a basic, accessible, and inclusive guide to spells for just about every purpose, as well as simple seasonal and life cycle rites. These are informed by my decades of experience and training; they avoid common mistakes and are based on a reliable, functional ritual structure that will hold you in good stead. You'll learn to work these rites as well as create your own. (Creativity, it turns out, is one of the most magical energies there is.)

The vast majority of Wiccans are solitary—you almost certainly practice alone. Most of these spells are designed with that in mind. Several, though, are written specifically for groups and couples. You may also adapt solitary workings to a group. These are *your* spells and you should make them work for *your* setting and situation. If you don't have a yard, use your garden spell with an indoor planter. If you use a wheelchair or other assistive device, modify walking spells to work with it. *You're* in charge of your magic; I'm just here to help!

In these pages, you'll find just about any spell you're looking for; from beginning to end, from love to courage, it's all here. Most importantly, you'll discover a guide to living a truly magical life.

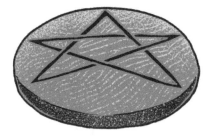

Stepping Into Wicca

Before we start casting spells, let's set the stage. It's helpful first to learn about the history of Wicca as it relates to spells, and it's vital to talk about ritual basics. You'll want to know how to prepare yourself for ritual, how to make yourself ready to cast a spell or perform a rite, and how to create a simple Wiccan circle. We'll also go over a basic supply list to be a truly well-stocked witch.

Spells and Wicca in History

Paganism—worshipping various Gods and Goddesses—is not the same as practicing witchcraft. In Wicca, the two come together.

The antecedents of Wiccan magical practice exist in several interesting places. First, Wicca is a descendant of the Western Mystery Tradition. This means that, believe it or not, all of those fancy old magicians with swords and triangles marked on the floor, paging through their grimoires written in Latin and Greek, are among the ancestors of our simple practice! We find traces of this heritage in the carefully cast circle, in the summoning of the "watchtowers" at the cardinal points, and in tools like the wand and athame.

But folk magic, too, is part of our history—the cunning man and wise woman in their huts on the outskirts of town, selling their charms and spells while something mysterious bubbles in the cauldron. From them, we inherit practicality, simplicity, herbalism, the use of runes, and more.

These two images from history are nearly opposite—one rich, one poor; one elaborate, one simple. Yet it's in the roots of these two that we meet in Wicca.

Wicca's earliest practitioners learned much of what they knew of spellcasting and magic from the Western Mystery Tradition, but Gerald Gardner, the founder of modern Wicca, wanted something easier to learn, a practice that was not expensive or elitist—folk magic. The coven he joined worked within both of these streams. And when he founded a coven of his own, the spells they did contained components of each.

Gardner was also fascinated by tribal religions and traveled extensively. In Malaysia, during the 1920s and 1930s, he met indigenous folk religionists who taught him the use and power of Spiritism, drumming, and healing work. This, too, was incorporated into his coven work.

The most famous historical Wiccan spell is known as "Operation Cone of Power." Gardner wrote that in 1940, witches worked to prevent Hitler from crossing the English Channel. Although some dispute the claim, it has been written about often, including in the novel *Lammas Night* by Katherine Kurtz. We can be proud of our rich heritage of multiple magical traditions as we busily create a diverse and inclusive magical future.

The Practice of Wicca

There are a few necessities to master in order to cast spells and create rituals. Not every spell you do involves a cast circle, but they all involve *you*, the witch. In the next few pages, we'll go over how to prepare yourself and your space, and how to cast a simple circle.

It is absolutely necessary that *you* are ready. That means you can calm yourself, you can bring forth memories at will, you can concentrate, and you can visualize (or form images using other senses—if you hear your goal rather than see it, that's fine).

The essential first step for all of these is meditation. If you don't have a meditation practice, begin now, until you are comfortable clearing your mind and concentrating for 15 to 20 minutes at least twice a week.

The Well-Stocked Witch

A witchy cabinet of supplies is a side effect of doing magic. You're not going to the store to buy just one candle! Soon enough, through the course of your practice, you'll have a drawer, trunk, or shelf of magical goodies.

What do you actually *need*, though? People say the only essential magical tool is the mind. While that's true, "stuff" does a lot for a spell; just as you can walk but driving is faster, the accoutrements of magic get you there quicker.

MAGICAL TOOLS

These are permanent things that have symbolic power and are usually consecrated:

◆ A tool to direct power. This is an athame (the witch's double-edged knife), wand, or staff.

◆ A goblet or chalice. This holds water or wine used as an offering.

◆ A special pen for magical writing.

◆ Symbols of the four elements: the goblet or a seashell for Water, a feather or fan for Air, candles for Fire, and a stone for Earth.

ALTAR SUPPLIES

Permanent things for the altar that are practical and not necessarily consecrated:

◆ Some small dishes for salt, loose incense, and the like.

◆ An incense burner or censer.

◆ Candle holders.

◆ A fire extinguisher (essential!).

◆ The altar itself (usually a small table, but you can also use a shelf or a tray).

SPELL SUPPLIES

Things that get used up in the course of doing magic:

◆ Candles are your main supply. You'll eventually want a large variety of sizes and colors, but begin with simple white votives. White is a universal substitute for any color.

◆ Matches.

◆ Incense. Varieties approach infinity and are specific to their purposes. Start with an all-purpose purifier like frankincense or sandalwood.

◆ Charcoals (for use with loose incense).

◆ Thick, high-quality paper for writing spells.

◆ Sea salt.

Preparing Your Space

In your practice, you may choose more or less elaborate ways of doing ritual and spells. You may sometimes cast a circle far more ornate than the one I outline below. Other times, you may pull over to the side of the road, take a deep breath, and do a bit of mini-magic at an isolated rest stop. Regardless of how simple or complex your rite, these preparation steps are always vital.

SAFETY

Make sure your space is safe. If you're going to dance, check the floor for hazards. If you're lighting candles or incense, have a fire extinguisher handy.

PRIVACY

If you fear you will be interrupted, your mind cannot fully focus on the work at hand. Make sure your door is locked, the baby is asleep, and, if you have roommates, that they know not to disturb you. Turn off the phone and other screens. Don't schedule something for right after you finish—inevitably, that will make you rush and in turn dilute the power of your rite.

INGREDIENTS AND SUPPLIES

Do an inventory of any ingredients and supplies needed for your spell before you begin, so you don't have to stop in the middle to fetch something.

Preparing Your Body

How you prepare is up to you. There are many options to consider. You can anoint with oil, bathe or splash with consecrated water, or cense with sage or cedar to cleanse yourself. Change out of your street clothes, whether to be skyclad (naked) or to put on a robe or some other special garb or jewelry reserved for magic. These steps cue your mind to focus on the work you're about to do.

CENTERING

Breathe deeply and connect to your center before any work begins.

GROUNDING

Connect to Mother Earth. Send your centered energy deep into Her loving soil.

MERGING

When working in a group, send your centered, grounded energy to each other, becoming one before you begin.

Choose to Do Right

Contrary to popular opinion, the Wiccan Rede "An it harm none, do as you will" is *not* a universal Wiccan law. ("Rede" means "advice," not law.) The God and Goddess are within us. We know, without being handed any law, what is right and what is wrong. Because we walk with the Gods, we choose to do right, and to seek wisdom and guidance within.

Wicca is a religion that venerates Mother Earth. All of your magic should, naturally, be consistent with the values of respect for life, respect for the Earth, and living in balance with nature. When you make a commitment to Wicca, you take on an obligation to behave ethically as part of your path.

There's *so much* healing and love needed in the world—focus on that and you'll be fine.

Creating the Magic Circle

There are dozens of Wiccan traditions, each with its own take on how a circle is cast. These don't even include the rituals countless scores of people have developed on their own.

I've been using the steps below for over 35 years. They work, they flow logically, they're not overly complex, and they create a powerful place in which to worship the Gods and Goddesses and perform spells. Your own steps may be different. Still, these can serve as blueprints should you choose to use them.

Begin by setting up an altar in the center (see the illustration on page 4). Have a lit candle at each quarter.

DECLARE INTENTION

State why you are here: "*I open this circle to worship the Gods,*" or "*This circle will be opened and magic will be done,*" or whatever is appropriate.

CONSECRATE AND COMBINE THE ELEMENTS

Elements are consecrated by concentrating energy into them, usually with your athame or wand, while stating something like, "*I do consecrate this [element] in the name of the Lady and Lord.*"

Consecrate incense (Air) and a lit charcoal (Fire), then combine them on the censer. Consecrate water (Water) and salt (Earth), and mix them. You now have four sacred elements.

CAST THE CIRCLE

Walk to the East. Using your athame or wand, draw the circle as you walk deosil (clockwise), ending where you began. Say, "*This is a circle, a sacred place, a protected place, a place of power. So mote it be!*"

CLEANSE AND CHARGE THE CIRCLE

Sprinkle the saltwater deosil, from East to East, to cleanse the circle, then bring the incense censer from East to East to charge the circle.

CALL THE QUARTERS

In the East, point your athame or wand in salute, and say: "*I call Air to guard this sacred circle in the East! Blessed be!*"

In the South, point your athame or wand in salute, and say: "*I call Fire to guard this sacred circle in the South! Blessed be!*"

In the West, point your athame or wand in salute, and say: "*I call Water to guard this sacred circle in the West! Blessed be!*"

In the North, point your athame or wand in salute, and say: "*I call Earth to guard this sacred circle in the North! Blessed be!*"

Return to the East and salute. The circle is now cast.

INVOKE THE GODS

Invite the God and Goddess you worship to join you. Use your own words: descriptive, heartfelt, and sincere. Thank them for coming and say, *"Blessed be!"*

GIVE AN OFFERING

Honor the Gods and Goddesses and thank them for coming by making an offering. Sing, recite a poem of praise, dance, drum, etc.

CAKES AND WINE

Consecrate wine or juice by plunging your athame or wand into the full cup. Then consecrate cake or bread by sprinkling it with the consecrated drink. Set aside some of each as an offering to be left outdoors later, then enjoy some yourself.

You are now ready to perform magic. You can also simply enjoy being in the circle with the Gods.

Closing the Magic Circle

Always close the circle. Never leave energies to just hang around. Loose energies can create mischief or even harm. Finish what you've begun by reversing each step. Closing also helps you return to normal consciousness, and keeps you grounded, balanced, and healthy.

Closing a circle is "last in, first out." If you use a different order than the one I've defined here, follow your own order, in reverse.

Some people go around counterclockwise (widdershins) to close the circle, but I do not. Widdershins is a powerful way of unwinding something; closing the circle is a lot easier than that!

THANK THE GODS AND SAY FAREWELL

Thank the God and Goddess you worship for joining you. As with your invocation, use your own words: descriptive, heartfelt, and sincere. Thank them for coming and say, *"Blessed be!"*

THANK EACH QUARTER

Go in the same order, East, South, West, North. Point your athame or wand in salute, say thank you and farewell. Then return for a final salute in the East.

UNCAST THE CIRCLE

Walk once around the perimeter of the circle, declaring the circle is over and all is as it was before.

DECLARE THE CIRCLE CLOSED

A traditional phrase is, *"The circle is over and the rites are ended. Merry meet, merry part, and merry meet again."*

So Mote It Be

At this point, we've gone through a lot of preliminary steps, and can spend the rest of this book on the meaty stuff—spells, magic, and other rites. We've covered a touch of history, reviewed supplies, and sketched out the basic steps of casting and closing a circle. Without a doubt, each of these things could be a bookshelf in itself, but our purpose is spells, and we're ready to get to it.

The following chapters will be grouped by the intention of each spell: beginnings, love and friendship, endings, and so on. There's also a chapter specifically for groups and couples.

Remember that these spells belong to you. They're yours to explore with, to tweak, to learn from, even to reject if one or another doesn't speak to you. A witch is a person of power, so grab your power and dive in!

CHAPTER 2

Spells of Beginning

Maria von Trapp was right—the beginning is a very good place to start. Life is full of beginnings and endings, and Wicca marks life cycles with great attention.

This chapter will have several different kinds of beginnings: first, starting out in the Craft and as a witch; then spells that create, bless, empower, or soothe new beginnings; and finally, life cycle rituals to honor beginnings.

The Beginning of Witchcraft

These are spells and rituals that help
establish a practice of Wicca.

To Consecrate Magical Tools

I mentioned earlier that it's best to consecrate tools. Here's how to do that.

SUPPLIES

- The tool to be consecrated

- Statues/symbols
  of the God and
  Goddess [optional]

- Something that's already
  consecrated [optional]

NOTES

- If you don't have loose
  incense, stick can be used.
  The Air consecration is
  done on the stick, and the
  Fire consecration is done
  when you light it.

- If you have an already
  consecrated tool,
  have it on the altar,
  touching the new tool,
  so that the consecration
  is "contagious."

STEPS

1. Cast the circle (page 7).

2. Lift your new tool to the statues of the God and Goddess
   (or visualize Them in your mind's eye), and say:

   *"Lady and Lord, bless the work of consecration
   I will do."*

3. Pass the tool through the incense smoke thoroughly,
   touching all parts of it with smoke, and say:

   *"I do consecrate this [tool] by Air and by Fire, that it
   be used with intelligence and passion. So mote it be!"*

4. Wet the tool with the saltwater thoroughly, touching all
   parts of it, and say:

   *"I do consecrate this [tool] by Water and Earth, that it
   be used with love and commitment. So mote it be!"*

5. Lift the tool to the God and Goddess, and say:

   *"Lady and Lord, bless this holy [tool] that it may be
   used in Your honor. So mote it be!"*

6. Use the tool immediately. Once finished, close the circle
   (page 8).

How to Dress a Candle

Dressing a candle immediately before using it in any spell adds energy.

SUPPLIES

- An essential oil consistent with the purpose of your spell, such as patchouli for lust or grounding, vervain for love or peace, or peppermint for psychic abilities [optional]

- Any other ingredient consistent with your purpose, such as rose petals for love, or rosemary for memory [optional]

- Pure olive oil

- A candle

NOTES

- You're not infusing the oil, so, for example, rose petals won't impart their scent.

- Instead of an essential oil, you can also use a mixture, such as Luck and Money Oil (page 128).

STEPS

1. Add a few drops of essential oil, and any other ingredients you've chosen, to the olive oil.

2. Concentrating on your purpose, dip your fingers in the oil and coat the candle. For spells of growth, positivity, or new beginnings, go from the base, up and clockwise. For spells that decrease, diminish, or make things go away, go from the tip, down and counterclockwise.

3. Your candle is now dressed.

Finding a Personal God or Goddess

This is a spell to find a personal deity. Maybe They will become your lifelong patron, or maybe you will work together for a while and then repeat the spell. Not everyone in Wicca has a patron deity, but if you have that relationship, it is powerful. A patron deity can be demanding, even difficult, but can also be your guide through the darkest as well as the best of times. I have worked with mine for over 35 years.

SUPPLIES

- A gold, silver, or white candle, dressed (page 13)

- An encyclopedia of mythology, or of Gods and Goddesses

NOTES

- You can find the encyclopedia at the library; you don't have to own or buy it.

- Leave the room dark enough that the candle will draw your gaze, but not so dark that you can't read, or that you might knock over the candle inadvertently.

- Once you have the results of this spell, learn as much as you can about this God or Goddess, make offerings, and perhaps bless a statuette of Them (page 16).

STEPS

1. Light the candle.

2. With the book in your lap, sit and gaze at the candle. Allow yourself to be drawn into the flame. Breathing slowly and deeply, notice yourself becoming more intuitive, more in touch with yourself, more in touch with Spirit.

3. Allow yourself to ask, silently or aloud, in words or just in feelings, for your personal God or Goddess to come to you.

4. When you feel the moment is right, open the book and allow your dominant hand to fall anywhere on the page.

5. The God or Goddess name closest to your index finger is the answer to your prayer.

Creating a Personal Altar

Casting a circle is wonderful, but sometimes more elaborate than you want. It's great to have a place to simply meditate, pray, or do quick spells. This is where a personal altar comes in.

SUPPLIES

The supplies below are suggestions to spark your creativity:

- A tray, plate, box, or cloth to use as the altar's surface.

- Symbols of the elements. These don't have to be the same ones you use for circle casting. Instead of a goblet, a censer, incense, and salt, you could have a seashell, a candle, a feather, and a stone.

- Symbols of one or more deities.

- Something pleasing to Them, such as a peacock feather for Hera.

- A symbol of presence, such as a bell or a crystal, that connotes, "I am here."

- A concentration aid, such as prayer beads or a candle.

STEPS

1. Prepare a clean, beautiful spot for your altar.

2. Arrange your altar so that it pleases you.

3. Using your symbol of presence, bring yourself fully to the moment. Say, *"I am here, before my altar."*

4. Using your concentration aid, mentally surround yourself and your altar with a glowing egg of light. Know that your altar is there for you to use, for prayers and spells, whenever you need it.

5. Say, *"Blessed be,"* and put your things back on the altar until next time.

To Bless a Statuette or Symbol of a God

Blessing a symbol of a deity is a beautiful way to know that the God or Goddess is present with you during rituals. The symbol can be a statue, a framed picture, something from nature associated with the deity (such as a seashell, antler, feather, or branch), or something from that deity's folklore.

Research your God or Goddess before this rite, both to increase the descriptive power of your invocation and to choose an appropriate offering. You can use this format for any deity and reuse it for multiple deities. For this example, I use Selene, a Goddess of the moon.

SUPPLIES

- Your chosen deity symbol

- An already consecrated statue [optional]

- An invocation that you've written for this deity

- An appropriate offering for this deity

NOTES

- If you have an already consecrated statue, use the idea of "magical contagion" just as you did when consecrating a tool (page 12).

- Not all deities have names that are known. You can, for example, use a title to bless a prehistoric deity image.

STEPS

1. Cast the circle (page 7).

2. Pass the statue through the incense smoke, touching all parts of it with smoke, and say:

   "Statue, be blessed by Air and by Fire, to be a fit home for Selene's worship."

3. Wet the statue with the saltwater thoroughly, touching all parts of it, and say:

   "Statue, be blessed by Water and Earth, to be a fit home for Selene's worship."

4. Visualize the Goddess. Imagine all Her divine attributes. See Her filling the statue as you invoke:

   "I call You, lovely Selene, to bless this statue
   with Your presence
   Lady of the Moon, wise One
   Come, be worshipped
   Come, be loved
   You who ride the silver chariot
   Daughter of Hyperion
   Come, be here
   Come, be adored!
   So mote it be!"

5. As you finish your invocation, envision a glow surrounding the statue. Feel confident that you have succeeded and that the Goddess is present.

6. Immediately make an appropriate offering, suited to the deity, and say something like:

   > *"Beloved Selene, accept this moon cake made in Your honor."*

7. Proceed with closing the circle (page 8).

Life Cycle Rituals: Beginning a New Phase

Life cycle rituals mark major passages.
All religions mark birth, death, and important
phases in between, and Wicca is no different.

Life Passage Rite Template

Here's a magical "template" for a life passage, which we'll fill in with subsequent rites (such as a Baby Blessing, page 22). You'll find this template useful in the future, when creating rites for your own special occasions. The example here is for a coming-of-age ceremony.

Decorate the altar with symbols of the occasion, and make everything special—your fanciest candleholder, your most beautiful altar cloth. The color of your altar candles should match the occasion (red for anything related to birth or rebirth, black for death, and so forth).

SUPPLIES

Vary by the specific rite

STEPS

1. Cast the circle (page 7). You can invoke deities specific to the type of event (birth, travel, marriage, etc.), or your usual Lady and Lord.

2. After cakes and wine, announce the work to be done. Ask the Lady and Lord to bless it.

   Example:
   "Tonight, we are here to celebrate Willow's coming of age. Tonight, Willow ceases to be a child and becomes a young woman.
   Lady and Lord, look upon Willow with love. Empower our work tonight and accept the new, adult Willow in your embrace."

3. Bless the subject of the work. Use both words and symbols. Giving a gift is typical.

> Example:
> *"Willow, the child is no more. I bless the woman you have become."*

Anoint Willow with oil.

Give Willow a special bracelet made by her parents, with symbols from her babyhood as well as of adulthood.

> *"Willow, this bracelet symbolizes adulthood. You will carry your childhood with you, but it will no longer be you. Wear it with love and honor."*

4. If the subject is present, have them participate. If the subject cannot participate (a rite for the departed, a rite for a baby), have one or more people speak on their behalf.

> Example:
> *Willow now speaks about the adult she intends to be, perhaps thanks the community, and makes an offering to the Gods.*

5. Present the subject of the rite to each quarter. Return to the East to complete the circle with a silent acknowledgment.

> Example:
> *"Guardian of the East/South/West/North, I present Willow, now an adult. Blessed be."*

6. Return to the altar and announce the rite is complete.

> Example:
> *"It is done. Willow is now a woman in our community. So mote it be!"*

7. Celebrate!

8. Close the circle (page 8).

Rite of Dedication to Wicca

Initiation is a rite of entry into a group. It's not something you do alone—you're brought in by others. Dedication, though, can be done in a group or entirely alone. You are *dedicated* to a path and to the Gods.

This is a big step, both joyful and solemn. Fast for a full day in preparation and spend extra time on your ritual cleansing. The words should come from your heart. Mine in the spell below are only examples.

SUPPLIES

- Red altar candles

- A new necklace symbolizing your dedication

NOTES

- Since you're dedicating to Wicca, you should perform the rite in an out-of-doors cast circle. If this is impossible, for reasons of privacy, spend time in meditation outdoors before the rite.

- Red candles are used for most life passages, as red symbolizes the blood of life.

- Use the Life Passage Rite template for steps 4 through 8 (page 18).

STEPS

1. Cast the circle (page 7).

2. Tell the Lady and Lord why you're taking this step. Ask Them to accept you as Their child.

3. Say:

    "I dedicate myself to the path of Wicca."
    Touch your feet, breast, and forehead with saltwater, and say:
    "By Water and Earth I am a witch ever more."
    Cense your feet, breast, and forehead, and say:
    "By Fire and Air I am a witch ever more."
    Put on your necklace, and say:
    "This necklace of dedication is my promise of a life in service to the Lady and Lord."

4. Continue to steps 4 through 8 of the template, filling in appropriate words; you are a dedicant, Wiccan, and witch.

Rite of Taking a Magical Name

In Wicca, it is typical to have a "Pagan" or "Witch" name. Some use it only in ritual, and some use it whenever among Pagan folk. This name represents who you choose to be as a Wiccan; it can describe who you are, or it can be aspirational.

SUPPLIES

◆ Red altar candles

NOTES

◆ Because the name is a new "thing," a physical symbol or representation (like a necklace) isn't typically used.

◆ Use the Life Passage Rite template for steps 5 through 8 (page 18).

STEPS

1. Cast the circle (page 7).

2. Announce to the Lady and Lord that you are taking a new name, and that henceforth you'll be known in the circle by this name. Ask Them to bless the name.

3. Say:

    "I am hereby [name]."
   Sprinkle and cense your feet, and say:
    "I enter the circle as [Name]."
   Sprinkle and cense your heart, and say:
    "I worship the Lady and Lord as [Name]."
   Sprinkle and cense your mouth, and say:
    "I speak the sacred words as [Name]."
   Sprinkle and cense your third eye, and say:
    "All that I know, I know as [Name]. So mote it be."

4. Speak about the meaning of the name. If it is a deity name, tell a story from the deity's mythology. Say what it means to you. Even alone, get into storytelling mode—you're introducing yourself.

5. Continue to steps 5 through 8 of the template, filling in appropriate words; at each step, use the new name. It is now your name.

Baby Blessing Rite

The best way to do this joyous rite is with a loving group of friends and family. Such a rite is often called a "Paganing" or "Wiccaning," bringing the new child into the community. The blanket in this blessing represents the baby being "blanketed" in the love of the Gods. It can be homemade or store-bought. If a group participates, everyone in the group can add something personal and magical, with embroidery, appliqué, or the like. This ritual is based on the legend of Sleeping Beauty—wherein every witch blesses the baby with a gift.

SUPPLIES

- Red altar candles
- A new baby blanket

NOTES

- If necessary, you may do this rite alone, with or without the baby. The rite will still be effective and meaningful.
- Use the Life Passage Rite template for steps 6 through 8 (page 18).

STEPS

1. Cast the circle (page 7).

2. Lift the baby in your arms, and say:

   "We are here to bring [name] into the loving embrace of the Gods and the community of Wicca. Lady and Lord, bless this work, that [name] will ever be under your divine protection."

3. Pass the baby over the smoke, and say:

   "Blessed be [name] with intelligence and strong will."
   Sprinkle the baby with saltwater, and say:
   "Blessed be [name] with love and stability."
   Wrap the baby in the blanket, and say:
   "Blessed be [name] with the love of all of us, and the protection of the Lady and Lord. So mote it be."

4. Each person in the ritual now steps forward and blesses the baby with a quality, such as *"I bless you, [name] to be a good listener,"* or *"I bless you with athleticism."* They kiss the baby and return to their place.

5. Carry the baby to each quarter:

> "[Name], this is the East. Here things are born. Here,
> you learn to think. Guardians of the East, watch
> over [name].
> [Name], this is the South. Here things become strong.
> Here, you learn power. Guardians of the South, watch
> over [name].
> [Name], this is the West. Here things are dreamed.
> Here, you learn to love. Guardians of the West, watch
> over [name].
> [Name], this is the North. Here things die, but that
> won't happen to you for a very long time. Here, you
> learn to be patient. Guardians of the North, watch
> over [name]."

Return to the East.

6. Continue to steps 6 through 8. The baby is blessed.

Creating, Blessing, and Empowering Beginnings

These are spells to create new things in life, and to deal with new things when they begin.

First Day at School: A Spell for Parents

Your child's first day at school is a joyous beginning, and a time of letting go. Perform this spell the day before that momentous occasion.

SUPPLIES

- Bubbles (enough for everyone)

NOTES

- You can do this alone, with your child, with your partner, or all three.

STEPS

1. If your child is present, explain what you're doing. Explain that the bubbles are flying, and they're so happy, and when they burst, they burst from happiness, but their beautiful energy is still out there, flying to wonderful heights.

2. Dip the bubble wand, and say:

   "These bubbles are [child's name], and this bubble wand is me [or us, for both parents], sending [child's name] off on a wonderful new adventure!"

3. Blow bubbles together. As you do, say:

   "Off you go [child's name]!
   Fly high!
   You're doing great at school!"

4. Repeat this several times. Have fun with it. Sing it, shout it, run around as you send the bubbles off. Let the energy dissipate easily into play, until everyone is laughing and tired.

First Day on the Job

You want to start off a new job on the right foot, but you don't necessarily want people at work to see you practicing witchcraft on day one. This spell lets you bless the first day of a new job discreetly but effectively.

SUPPLIES

- A portable container into which you've mixed the consecrated saltwater and ashes from previous rituals

NOTES

- The spell is written for an office but can be adapted to wherever or however you work.

- Perform this spell on your first day, regardless of the moon phase. If your place of work is too crowded for discretion, wait until a waxing moon and arrive extra-early, so that other people aren't around.

- If you just wet your fingers and shake the drops off, you'll likely go unnoticed.

STEPS

1. When you arrive at work, sprinkle a few drops of the mix onto your feet (for instance, as you are getting out of the car), and say:

   "Bless my first steps."

2. If possible, as you enter the building, sprinkle a few drops on the threshold, and say:

   "Bless my entrance."

3. At your new desk, stand and visualize yourself surrounded by glowing white light. Sprinkle the mix in a circle around you, and say:

   "Bless this beginning. Bless this place of work. So mote it be."

Bless My New Home

This spell removes negative energy and brings positivity to a new home. You can also use this spell on a home that isn't new, if you're new to magic and unlikely to move anytime soon.

SUPPLIES

- Your athame or wand
- A dish of saltwater

NOTES

- This spell is best performed at the first waxing moon upon moving in, at dawn or twilight.

- This spell is designed to work for an apartment or an attached home. If it's a house, you can perform step 1 (banishing) and step 2 (blessing) outdoors first. Then proceed with the spell indoors.

STEPS

1. Starting at the front door of your new home, move widdershins to each door, window, and any other opening (such as a fireplace). Stop at each, point your athame or wand, concentrate on pushing energy outward, and say:

   "I banish negativity from this place! All that can harm me, be gone! So mote it be!"

2. Now return to the front door. This time, move deosil. At each threshold, at every windowsill, and at other openings, sprinkle saltwater. Visualize white, clear, sparkling light, full of good feelings, flowing from the saltwater, and say:

   "I bless this place. Be cleansed, be purified, be beautified. So mote it be!"

3. Finish by sprinkling the front threshold a second time, and say:

   "My home is blessed. I am welcome here."

Charm for Starting a Project

Whether you're writing a book, learning peyote beading, or starting a lactation support group, every endeavor needs a bright beginning. This charm will help empower whatever you start.

SUPPLIES

- A stone that you will acquire during the course of the spell

NOTES

- Perform this spell at sunrise on the first morning after a new moon.

- Find a spot where dew gathers on grass or other greenery. Scope the location in advance, to ensure the sunrise is visible and that you will be there in time to witness it.

STEPS

1. Face East and close your eyes. Inhale deeply, and say:

   "Air of inspiration, let us begin."

2. Open your eyes and see the sunrise. Say:

   "Fire of dawn, I take you in."

3. Look around. Pick up the first stone you see.

4. Face West and gently drag the stone through the greenery, wetting it with morning dew. Say:

   "Water, bless the work I do."

5. Look at your stone, and say directly to it:

   "Earth power makes it true."

6. Pocket the stone, and say:

   "So mote it be."

7. Keep the stone with you whenever you're working on your project.

Spell for Fertility

Even more than healing, love, or money, fertility seems to be the magic people seek the most, and it is among the most ancient of magics. It's also very effective! Naturally, it's best when combined with seeing a doctor, as well as looking within to find and release any psychic barriers.

SUPPLIES

- Your athame or wand
- A pot full of potting soil for planting
- Whole mustard seeds, in a small dish
- A drum, rattle, or other simple musical instrument

NOTES

- Perform this spell during a full or waxing moon.
- You can perform this spell for yourself or for another, working alone or in a group. If you do have a group, familial energy is ideal.
- If the subject of the spell isn't present, have a consecrated picture on the altar.
- Mustard is a cool-weather plant, suitable for early spring in a temperate zone, or indoor growth, and is harvested in 30 to 40 days.

STEPS

1. Cast the circle (page 7). You should invoke a Goddess of fertility, such as Hera, Freya, or Danu.

2. After cakes and wine, consecrate the soil, planting your athame in it, and say:

   "O fertile earth, the seeds I plant will grow and grow.
   O fertile earth, make [name/me] fertile that [her/my] seeds may grow and grow.
   O fertile earth, O fertile earth
   Bringer of new life
   Bring new life to [name/me]."

3. Consecrate the seeds, pointing your athame in the dish, and say:

   "Seeds bring forth life!
   Seeds bring forth life!
   As you grow, so grows [her/my] womb, full of life!
   As you grow, so grows [her/my] womb, full of life!"

4. Now dance and/or make music, building an intense tempo, increasing energy and intensity until it is almost unbearable. Visualize the target of your spell happily pregnant, glowing with health. As you reach peak, *thrust* all your energy into the soil and seeds, while holding that image in your head.

5. Plant the seeds, and say:

   "So mote it be!"

6. Close the circle (page 8).

7. Care for the plant. As it grows, fertility will grow.

Trunk Party Spell for Success in College

When my eldest nephew started college, my sister held a "trunk party" for him, filling his trunk with things he'd need for his dorm. Why not do the same thing for someone you love, except magically? This spell can be adapted for any occasion when "going away" or "new endeavor" gifts have been given.

SUPPLIES

- Colored paper and tape, or colored sticky notes
- A pen and scissors
- Gifts received from relatives and friends
- A trunk or suitcase

NOTES

- Shapes that could be meaningful are hearts for love, arrows for action, stars for inspiration, birds for hopes for the future, books for knowledge, and moons for dreams. Use your imagination!

STEPS

1. For each gift, choose a color and simple shape representing the person who gave it to you. Make a paper cutout of the shape and write the person's name on it. For example, a gift from Mom represents love—cut a heart out of pink paper and write "Mom" on it. Attach a paper label to each gift.

2. With your hands, send energy into the stack of labeled gifts.

3. Pick each up, in turn, and say something simple about it as you place it in the trunk or case. For example:

   "Mom sends me to college with love. I will succeed because of her love."
   Each statement is your own, individual and sincere. Each affirms success.

4. Once everything is in the trunk or case, and say:

   "Success is mine. So mote it be!"

5. Close the trunk.

Spells of Love and Friendship

Matters of the heart: They give us life's greatest joys, but also endless angst. The spells in this chapter are positive, healing, hopeful, and overflowing with the possibilities of love.

Spells of New Love

These spells bring love and friendship into your life,
focusing on and attracting love energy.

Bring the Person of My Dreams

This spell brings the person you imagined in the "What Do I Want?" spell
(page 33).

SUPPLIES

- Incense containing rose, thyme, lemon balm, and/or valerian

- Small red and pink candles (something that will burn down quickly)—seven of each

- Your final list from the "What Do I Want?" spell

NOTES

- A cast circle is optional here, but I prefer it. Should you choose to cast, invoke a Goddess of love, like Aphrodite or Hathor.

- Do this spell on a Friday during a waxing moon.

STEPS

1. Place the 14 candles into a heart shape that surrounds you. Light the candles, alternating between colors—light one pink and say *"For love,"* then one red and say *"For passion,"* continuing until all the candles are lit.

2. After cakes and wine (if you've cast a circle), consecrate your list with Air, Fire, Water, and Earth. Ask the Goddess to bless this work.

3. Now read your list out loud, preceding each item with "Lady send me," as in:

   "Lady, send me a woman who is available and ready for love . . ."
   "Lady, send me someone who lives nearby . . ."

4. Mentally send all your energy into this prayer. Continue to send energy until the candles burn all the way out, then say: *"So mote it be."*

What Do I Want?

A big barrier to finding love is that we often don't know what we want. Then, when we meet someone, we can't decide if they're right for us. This spell helps bring clarity to your new love prospect.

SUPPLIES

- Incense containing rosemary and/or rose

- A white candle, a red candle, and a pink candle, each dressed (page 13)

- Your magical writing pen and seven pieces of paper

NOTES

- Repeat this spell every night for seven nights, ending on, or the day before, the full moon. (Seven is the number of Venus, so many love spells use that number.)

- Each night of a multi-night spell requires the same preparation steps.

STEPS

1. Light the incense. Inhale deeply.

2. Light the white candle, and say: *"For clarity."*

3. Light the pink candle, and say: *"For love."*

4. Light the red candle, and say: *"For passion."*

5. Now simply ask yourself what you want, and begin making a list. Start with the basics—specify the gender or genders, or gender expression, you're attracted to (if that matters to you). It might start something like:

   A man who is available and ready for love
   . . . who lives nearby
   . . . who has a good job
   . . . who is into Star Wars . . .

6. When you feel your list is complete, put out the candles. Fold the paper and sleep with it under your pillow.

7. On nights 2 through 6, light the candles as before. Read your list and meditate on it for several minutes. Each night, rewrite it on a fresh sheet of paper, removing everything that is not essential and adding anything you've forgotten.

8. Each night, put out the candles and sleep with the new folded paper under your pillow.

9. Night 7 is the same, except this time, declare your spell complete and allow the candles to burn all the way down.

Spell to Get Invitations

Here is a spell designed to improve your social life. Don't do this if you don't want to go out! Once you've cast a spell releasing that desire into the world, you should accept appropriate invitations when they come.

SUPPLIES

+ A box of thank-you notes, opened ahead of time

+ Enough stamps for the whole box

+ Your magical writing pen

NOTES

+ Perform this spell in a cast circle during a waxing moon, on a Wednesday or Sunday.

STEPS

1. Cast the circle (page 7).

2. Consecrate the box of notes as you would a magical tool (page 12).

3. Touch your athame or wand to the box, and say:

   "I send my power into these notes
   They attract friendship to me
   They attract welcome to me
   They attract fun to me
   So mote it be!"

4. Now write a thank-you in each note. They should say something like:

   Thank you for the lovely invitation! I'll definitely be there.

   Sign your name, put it in an envelope, and seal it. Repeat until every note is used.

5. Address each envelope to a nonexistent address in your town or one nearby, and stamp it (don't use a return address).

6. Close the circle (page 8) and mail the notes as soon as possible, preferably the next morning.

First-Date Charm

First dates can be terrifying, so try carrying this charm with you. It doesn't guarantee true love; if this isn't the right person for you, you'll find out with a minimum of drama. But if it *is* the right person—yowza!

SUPPLIES

- A bind rune you created (page 36)
- Blue paper
- Your magical writing pen
- A pair of scissors

NOTES

- Blue represents calm, while the bind rune brings you happiness and love. Circles represent wholeness.

STEPS

1. Visualize your intention clearly: a relaxed, happy date going well. Picture laughter and ease. Feel a glow surrounding the two of you.

2. While visualizing, write your bind rune on the paper.

3. Draw a circle around the rune, and then carefully cut the paper along the circle.

4. Continue visualizing and trace the rune over and over, sending energy into it. Ignore the original characters and trace the new symbol. You can recite a simple chant as you write, such as *"Love and peace."* There is no set number of repetitions—do it as many times as feels right, ending with, *"So mote it be."*

5. Fold the paper and wear it in your shoe during the date.

How to Create a Bind Rune

A "bind rune" is a magical symbol of great power, because you've created it yourself. The technique comes from Norse magic, where you bind two or more characters from the Futhark alphabet together. But you don't have to confine yourself to Futhark. Bind runes can be used for virtually any purpose, marking magical or mundane objects with your intention.

SUPPLIES

◆ Regular paper and pen

NOTES

◆ In addition to *writing* a bind rune, you can consider using a technique, like embroidery, paint, or beading, which can become a creative, empowering, and meaningful part of your spells.

STEPS

1. Find two or three symbols that are meaningful to you. Often, one represents a magical goal (love, peace, riches) and the other represents the subject of the goal (your initial). In this example, we're using the Futhark rune *wunjo* for joy, and an astrological glyph for Taurus, to represent the birth sign of the subject. They combine to bring joy to a specific person.

2. Draw the symbols one on top of the other, until you have an aesthetically pleasing, and unique, symbol.

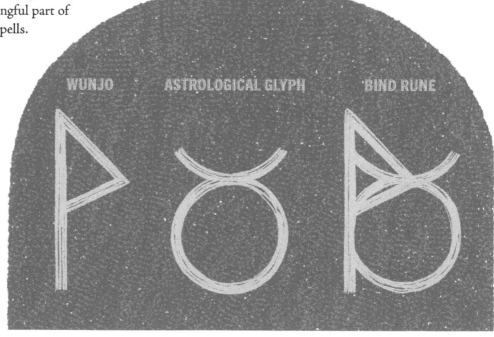

WUNJO   ASTROLOGICAL GLYPH   BIND RUNE

DRAW YOUR BIND RUNES

Spells for Existing Relationships

Maybe a spell for new love isn't what you need.
If you're already in a relationship, it can be powerful
to use your witchcraft to help and heal that relationship.

Bless This Romance

This spell is meant to stabilize a new romance that you *both* want to have a future. It's not intended to be, and should not be, a one-sided spell. Don't use it to bless a "romance" that you feel but the other person doesn't (or doesn't yet) reciprocate entirely.

SUPPLIES

- A bead representing each person (see Notes for guidance on choosing a bead)

- Brown or green thread (representing Earth, stability, and commitment)

- Incense and a small dish of saltwater

NOTES

- Birthstones are precious gems, but they also represent color correspondences. Instead of emerald, for example, any green stone can represent a Taurus. When selecting stones, consider using an inexpensive stone of the same color as each person's birthstone.

- Perform the spell on a Saturday during a waxing moon.

STEPS

1. Pass your bead through the incense, then the saltwater, and say:

   "By Air and Fire/by Water and Earth, This is me in relation to [partner's name]."

2. Now pass your partner's bead through the incense, then the saltwater, and say:

   "By Air and Fire/by Water and Earth, This is [partner's name] in relation to me."

3. Now pass the thread through the incense, and say:

   "Air binds our minds to Earth. Fire binds our passion to Earth."

4. Now wet the thread in saltwater, and say:

   "Water binds our hearts to Earth. Earth holds us together."

5. Thread the two beads together on the string and make seven knots. With each knot, say:

   "We are blessed."

6. Take the beads outside and find a secret place to bury them.

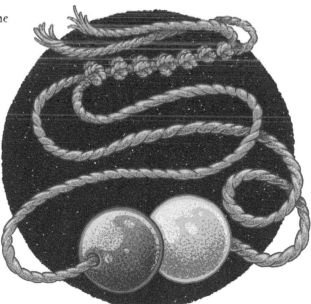

Bring Us Together

This is a spell to bring long-distance lovers together, spread over 10 nights' time. Should you choose to cast this spell, you should already be in love and committed, but living far apart; this spell helps you find a path to cohabitation or living in closer proximity.

SUPPLIES

- Saltwater and incense (lavender or lemongrass if possible), first night only, for consecration

- A map, showing where each of you lives (a printout or something you create yourself)

- Scissors and tape

- Your magical writing pen

NOTES

- Perform this spell during a waning moon: You are *diminishing* distance.

STEPS

1. Mark each of your locations on the map with a hand-drawn star.

2. Consecrate the map as you would a magical tool (page 12).

3. Slice the entire map in two, and cut away a piece of the distance between you. Tape the map back together, and say:

   "We are coming closer together. So mote it be."

4. Repeat step 3 every night.

5. On the 10th night, cut away all the remaining distance: When you tape it together, the stars should touch each other. Say:

   "We are together. So mote it be."
   Fold the map so that the stars are on the inside.

6. Take the map outside and burn it (safely). The ashes that scatter fly to your joint destiny, bringing you together. If you can't burn it outside, burn it safely indoors and scatter the ashes later.

Turn Me On!

This spell reawakens sexual passion either in a relationship or within yourself. It's designed for an otherwise healthy relationship. (Libido issues can be related to physical or emotional illness, and that should not be ignored.)

SUPPLIES

- A red candle, dressed (page 13), in a glass container (so it doesn't go out)

- A fiery food or drink known in folklore to be an aphrodisiac, such as hot peppers, whiskey, ginger candies or ginger drinks, or anything cardamom-infused or -flavored

NOTES

- Perform this spell on a Friday, when you can be exposed to hot sunlight.

- If you can't tolerate spices, some mild alternatives are strawberries, red wine, or pomegranate—but spicy is best. You want to bring heat to your life.

- Do not perform this spell during adolescence or other times of rapid hormone shifts (such as mid-gender transition or pregnancy).

STEPS

1. Take your candle and food outside on a sunny day, somewhere you can sit and meditate.

2. Gaze at the lit candle and imagine the fire coming into you, filling you. Feel it explicitly inflaming your groin and arousing you. Say:

   "I am fire. I am hot."

3. Eat or drink your aphrodisiac. Feel the heat of it going into your body. Let your skin tingle. Let your whole body feel heat; not just your groin, but your nipples, your buttocks, the back of your neck—everywhere you experience pleasure. Let heat become a part of you. Again say:

   "I am fire. I am hot."

4. Take the candle home and place it near the bed.

5. Enjoy stimulation, including climax (alone or with your partner). Throughout, visualize the fire being a part of your body, keeping a flame alive within you. It is a part of you.

To Heal a Rift

Use this spell to help heal a rift between friends, family members, or lovers. One of the estranged or struggling pair can be you, or you can be doing this on behalf of others. This spell isn't a substitute for good communication but can facilitate and encourage it. If a couple isn't meant to be together, it won't force them together—what it can do, though, is bring them together for better communication, even during a break-up.

SUPPLIES

- Two white 12-inch taper candles

- A straight pin or pocket knife

- A picture of each of the estranged people

NOTES

- You can start this spell at any phase of the moon. Change your phrasing and your visualization, so that in a waxing moon you're healing and bringing harmony, and in a waning moon you're shrinking the misunderstanding until it disappears.

- Your chosen candle dressing (page 13) should match the moon phase—up and deosil for waxing, down and widdershins for waning.

STEPS

1. Before dressing the candles, use the knife or pin to carve each person's initials and astrological sign into their candle. Then dress each candle, concentrating on the candle *being* the person.

2. Place the candles, each with its picture, about two feet apart from each other. Light the candles.

3. Rub your hands together vigorously, to warm them and raise energy. Hold your hands out, palm forward, so that each is facing one of the candles.

4. Say:

   "[Name 1] and [Name 2] are apart, but they're coming closer together."

5. Repeat this over and over, concentrating and sending energy through your palms. Stop when you feel the energy fully released.

6. Move the candles a bit closer together after the last repetition and gaze at them for a few minutes before you put them out.

7. Repeat steps 2 through 8 each night until the seventh night.

- You will perform this spell over the course of seven nights, and all seven nights should be in the same moon phase (from new to full, or from full to new).

8. On the seventh night, at step 5, say:

    "[Name 1] and [Name 2] were apart. Now they're together."

9. When you move the candles, they should touch. Say:

    "So mote it be!"

10. Let the candles burn all the way down.

Letting Love Grow (a Polyamory Spell)

This spell is designed to bring new people into a relationship that is stable, where both partners are enthusiastically polyamorous. You can do this spell with your partner or alone. It involves playacting, and to raise the energy needed, you have to get into it; be theatrical. Express surprise and happiness. Halfway through the spell, you have to go outside to bring "fresh air" to the relationship.

SUPPLIES

- Materials to make three poppets (page 98)
- Saltwater and incense for consecrations

NOTES

- If you want another person to make a triad, make three poppets. If you're looking for another couple, or two single people, make four poppets. For another couple, start them connected the way you'll connect your own poppets.

STEPS

1. Make poppets for yourself, your partner, and the unknown person(s) you're seeking. Make sure the hearts are very strong, they're smiling, and colors associated with love and happiness are used.

2. Consecrate each poppet as you would a tool (page 12). Name each so that it *is* the person it represents.

3. Sew your partner's hands to yours: You are together in this. Reconsecrate the joined poppets as a couple, e.g.: *Jane and Marie are now and forever a couple. We are joined.*

4. Consecrate the needle and thread as well. (Once you've done this, it is a magical tool—store it with your magic stuff and don't use it for ordinary sewing.)

5. Take the poppets, needle, and thread outside.

6. Put the poppet of the unknown person(s) down.

7. Holding the couple poppet, say:

   "We're looking around for the right person/people."

8. Spin around, holding the poppets. Say: *"We're looking around."* Repeat it over and over, spinning in faster and faster circles, until you're shouting and dizzy, and finally fall down!

9. On the ground, "find" the poppet(s) you put down. Get excited and say:

   "We found you! We found you!"

10. Sew the poppets so that they're now all holding hands. Say *"Now we're together"* over and over as you sew, ending with *"So mote it be."*

11. Place the poppets on your personal altar where their smiling faces are frequently visible. You can leave them there until the right partner(s) are found.

Marriage Blessing

You may have been invited to say a few words at a wedding and you want to say something magical that won't freak out the more conservative guests. Perhaps you want to say something privately, alone, out in nature, to bless them. Maybe you want to write something to include with the wedding gift. This blessing offers all of this flexibility.

When you speak or write, fill this blessing with the energy of your magic, that the Lady and Lord bless the happy couple.

Love lasts when the Sun smiles down, blessing you
with brightness.
Love lasts when the Earth holds you up, blessing you
with a foundation.
Be blessed by the Sun and Earth.
Life is balance. Your marriage will be blessed with
balance, and sometimes it won't be fun.
The ups are more fun than the downs.
The richer is more fun than the poorer.
But in balance, you are always together. When the sun
rises, you are together. When the moon rises, you are
together. Darkness and light, morning and night, the
balance of life is yours to share.
Remember the inspiration of new love. Allow a breath
of fresh air to come to you when life exhausts you.
Remember your passion for each other. The flame
never goes out, if you remember to fan it.
Love with an open heart. Whether with joy or tears,
your hearts are for each other.
Love is safe. Make a home together, that you always
are each other's safe harbor in any storm.
The support of your friends and family helps sustain
all of us, and we are here for you.
Be blessed.

Family Love

Families can be a source of great joy . . . or not. Tension in even the healthiest family is normal, and these spells address family issues both magically and realistically.

One Big Happy Family

If a family get-together for a holiday or other occasion is a time of tension and stress, carry a charm such as this one to bring harmony during those trying times.

SUPPLIES

- A rose quartz bead
- Saltwater and incense for consecrations
- Consecrated water
- A chain or embroidery silk for the bead

NOTES

- You'll be using invisible writing in this spell. You can use your finger, but I like to use a bamboo chopstick, consecrated and set aside for this magical purpose.

- Where the spell says *"in my family,"* you can specifically name people, e.g., *"between George and me."*

STEPS

1. Create a three-part bind rune (page 36): something representing harmony, something representing family, and something representing yourself.

2. Consecrate the bead:

   "I consecrate you by Fire and Air / Water and Earth, to be a tool of harmony and peace in my family."

3. Write the bind rune on the bead in water, over and over, focusing on peace and harmony. Feel the energy of peace emanating from it.

4. When you feel you are ready, put the bead on the chain or embroidery silk and wear it immediately, at least for a moment.

5. Wear it at your family gathering.

Bless the Growing Family

While welcoming a new baby can be a sought-for joy, the change in dynamics can sometimes bring tension to a couple. If one of you has given birth to the baby, jealousy from the non-birthing partner is common, and new parents are often frazzled. This spell helps a loving couple remain happily connected as the family expands.

SUPPLIES

◆ A taper candle, dressed (page 13)

◆ Collage-making supplies: Magazines, stickers, pictures, glitter, fabric, or whatever your imagination allows, as well as scissors and glue

◆ Your magical pen

◆ Four sheets of construction paper or oak tag

NOTES

◆ The candle can be light blue for harmony, pink for love and affection, or brown for home and stability.

◆ This spell can be completed in one sitting, or can be an ongoing art project that builds energy as it is created over a period of days.

STEPS

1. Light the candle, meditating on family harmony and setting your intention.

2. Assemble collage components that represent each person in the relationship. For example, for myself, I might choose pictures of tattoos, my favorite Disney villain, James Bond, and a family picture. I'd sketch five sisters, add some pink glitter, and maybe pull a page from a book I've written. Perhaps I'd add a favorite earring that has lost its mate. Be both creative and meditative—there are no wrong choices! Develop three piles—for you, for your partner, and for the baby.

3. Draw an outline of yourself on the first sheet of paper. Assemble and glue your collage components inside the outline.

4. Repeat step 3 for your partner and the baby. Then cut out each around the outline.

5. Hold each cutout before your candle, stating that each is the person it represents. *"This is me,"* and so forth.

6. On the fourth sheet, glue components for you and your partner so that you overlap, touching each other, but leaving space between. Say: *"We are together. We remain together."* Speak from the heart, improvising words that are true about your relationship.

◆ You can modify this spell if family shape and size are changing in a different way.

7. Now glue in the third piece—the baby. Restate: *"We are together. We remain together."* Add: *"As we grow, we grow together. So mote it be."*

8. Allow the candle to burn out.

9. Consider having the final family picture framed, keeping it always as a reminder of your togetherness.

Keep Us Connected

Moving away is a part of life. We stay in contact through phone calls, letters, and social media, but experiencing true connection is a different matter. This spell keeps you connected to a beloved family member or friend who is moving away.

SUPPLIES

- A picture of the two of you
- Your magical writing pen
- A frame to fit the picture

NOTES

- Do this spell on a Sunday during a waxing moon.

STEPS

1. Take the picture and pen to a private location outdoors, after the moon is out.

2. Hold the picture up to the moon, and say:

   "Beloved Lady, this is [Name] and me
   Keep our bond strong
   Bless our connection to each other
   Keep us always in each other's lives.
   Blessed be."

3. Face East, and say:

   "By Air may we be ever in each other's thoughts. May we speak often."

4. Face South, and say:

   "By Fire, let our decisions include each other, and let us share our passions with each other."

5. Face West, and say:

   "By Water, may we ever feel love for each other. Let us remember each other."

6. Face North, and say:

    *"By Earth, may our bonds and our commitments
    hold true."*

7. Face East again, and say:

    "So mote it be."

8. Sit down and write a heartfelt inscription on the back of
   the photo.

9. Thank the Goddess.

10. When you get home, frame the picture. Give the framed
    picture as a going-away present.

Unrivalry

Siblings are complicated. They can be our best friends, our worst enemies, baffling strangers, or all of these things at once. The "To Heal a Rift" spell (page 42) can work for siblings as well as for friends or lovers, but perhaps it's not a rift. Perhaps you want to be connected and you're just not. Maybe you only see each other once a year at the holidays, and you'd like to have more of them in your life.

SUPPLIES

- Your magical writing pen
- A square piece of paper
- A small jar
- Honey
- A white or pink candle

NOTES

- This spell is my Wiccan variation on a traditional hoodoo "honey jar" spell.
- Do the spell on a Wednesday when the Sun is in Gemini (about May 20 through June 19, though it varies each year).

STEPS

1. Write a list of everything positive and interesting you know about your sibling. If I were writing about my younger brother, I might write, "*He's an attorney. He adores his children. He loves classic rock,*" and so on. If you don't know much, *find out*. This is a preliminary step; you don't need to use your magic pen for this.

2. Now collect a symbol for each thing on your list. For "classic rock," I might use a guitar pick. Everything has to be small enough to fit into your jar. If you can't think of a thing, you can use a picture, or a small piece of paper with a word on it, but put plenty of thought into it before resorting to that.

3. Cast a circle (page 7).

4. After cakes and wine, center yourself and meditate on your sibling. Form a clear picture in your mind of the relationship you want to have.

5. Using your magic writing pen, write your sibling's name on the paper, once per line, filling the page top to bottom.

6. Turn the paper 180 degrees and write your own name once per line, top to bottom, so that you and your sibling are interconnected.

7. Fold the paper toward you, turn, and repeat, until it is quite small. Place it in the jar.

8. Pick up your first symbol, describe it, and put it in the jar. You might say:

   "My brother loves rock 'n' roll. This is sweet to me." Do this for each symbol you've collected, ending with *"This is sweet to me"* each time.

9. Fill the jar with honey and seal it.

10. Stick the candle to the top of the jar and light it, again visualizing your harmonious relationship.

11. As the candle burns, the wax will drip all over the jar, helping seal it. Continue gazing as long as you feel appropriate.

12. You can close the circle (page 8) while the candle is still burning, but don't blow it out—allow it to burn all the way down.

13. Keep the jar in a hidden place, knowing it sweetens your relationship.

CHAPTER 4

Spells for Groups
or Pairs

W icca was born in covens and is often still thought
of that way. Yet the vast majority of Wiccans
today are solitary in practice—either because they haven't
yet found a group or simply by choice. If you're solo by
choice, that's great, and if you're looking for a group, may
your search be blessed.

When a group really jibes, the whole is truly greater than the sum of its parts. Great beauty, and great power, can be found. These spells are for covens as well as more loosely connected groups. The magic here honors both the joys and the frustrations of group work.

Coven Spells

These are spells intended for a group of people working together as a coven. In group work, it's essential to make sure you're all on the same page. Agree in advance on where you're sending energy and why. You should all agree enthusiastically to any spell and have a shared understanding of what you'll visualize during your spell work.

The Lighthouse Spell: Bringing New Members

This is a classic spell taught to me as "The Ribbon." I've also seen it as a "beacon," or "searchlight." The light of attraction shines above your group, bringing the right people to you, while the wrong people, or those less suited to your group, can't even see it.

SUPPLIES

◆ None, other than what you use to cast a circle

NOTES

◆ Discuss the chosen visualization in advance, so that all of you can hold it clearly in your mind during the rite.

STEPS

1. Cast the circle (page 7).

2. After cakes and wine, raise the cone of power (page 57).

3. As you raise the cone, visualize the cone as a lighthouse, with a beautiful beacon of light shining forth from it. The "ships" it guides are new witches, finding their way to you. This is a *positive* beam, and only the people meant to be with you can see it. They will find themselves drawn to you. If you have a Meetup, they'll show up. If you have a table at Pagan Pride, they'll drop by.

4. When the drop is called, send all your energy into the brightness and perfection of that light.

5. Close the circle (page 8).

Raising the Cone of Power

The "Cone of Power" contains the energy raised in a cast circle, built by a group and released on command. The technique is simple, and used often, because it works powerfully, without any tools or special planning.

SUPPLIES

◆ None, other than what you use to cast a circle

NOTES

◆ One person is the leader and will "call the drop." Their job is to sense the energy and release it at the right moment.

◆ The circle is a container, holding the cone of energy until it is sent at the drop.

◆ It's normal for energy to fade or wobble, then lift again. Don't worry, just let it build.

◆ To use the cone for worship, raise it as part of your offering. For magic, raise it after cakes and wine.

STEPS

1. In a cast circle (page 7), stand, holding hands.

2. Begin a slow chant you all like, as you start to slowly walk, then dance, around the circle deosil.

3. Gradually build the tempo of chant and movement, until you're practically running.

4. The leader calls "*Now!*" and everyone drops to the floor, sending all their energy into the cone.

5. The leader is responsible for *pushing* the energy out, to its target, as it is sent by everyone else.

Blessing a New Group

If you've formed or joined a new coven or grove of witches, a ritual such as this one, which formally creates and names the group, can be powerful.

    If you intend to welcome new members in the future, you can devise a ceremony of welcome for new members similar to this one. Buy or make extra tokens if that's the case.

SUPPLIES

- A charm or token on a cord (one per person) that will represent your group. For example, if you are "Moonshadow Grove," a crescent moon might be your token.

- A dish to hold the tokens in.

NOTES

- Everyone should use their magical name (page 21) if they have one.

STEPS

1. Cast the circle (page 7).

2. After cakes and wine, join hands. Take a moment to center. Look around. Enjoy that you share this space with one another.

3. Ask the Lady and Lord to bless this new group, using its name.

4. One of you says, "*We are Moonshadow.*" Everyone picks it up so that you're all chanting it together, hand in hand. You might start dancing around, but don't build to a full peak. Get the energy where it feels warm and juicy, but don't spend it all.

5. One person now says,

   > "*I am [name] and I bring [quality].*"
   > Example:
   > "*I am Willow and I bring joy/my singing voice/my love of the Gods.*"

6. That person takes a token and puts it around her neck. Everyone says "*Welcome [name].*"

7. Each person repeats these steps.

8. At the end, you can return to your "*We are Moonshadow*" chant. Let it turn into a celebration!

9. Close the circle (page 8).

Celebrating the Gods Within

I believe the Gods are within us *and* outside of us. We can worship Them in both ways. This rite combines a spell of self-empowerment with worship of the Gods within.

SUPPLIES

- Drums, rattles, and other percussion instruments (enough for everyone)

NOTES

- Because this is truly *worship* of the deity within, it belongs at the point of offering in circle casting (page 8), not after cakes and wine, where a spell would be.

STEPS

1. Cast the circle (page 7).

2. One person goes first. That person sits in the center or at the altar.

3. Begin a drumbeat or rhythm, while chanting the person's name. Everyone can chant it as feels best for them—you're not trying to write a song. For example, one person could be percussive with the name (e.g., *Wil! LOW! Wil! LOW!*) while another could sing it, and another could whisper. Harmonize, interweave your voices—whatever works for you. Think of the name-chant as a gift you are giving the person whose name you chant. See the God or Goddess within them, and celebrate them freely.

4. Let the drumming go on, peaking, filling the space, and then gradually subsiding. When it comes to a natural end, it's the next person's turn.

5. Continue like this until everyone has had a turn in the center.

6. Now it's the time for cakes and wine. Continue the circle, celebrating the experience you've just had, until it's time to close.

7. Close the circle (page 8).

Parting of Ways

If a beloved coven member moves away, consider the "Keep Us Connected" spell (page 50). Sometimes, though, a coven member leaves for more complicated reasons. If you're not on speaking terms, you're not going to do this rite. But if you're all committed to parting with decency and kindness, remembering that you were once lovingly connected, this provides an opportunity to honor that.

This rite has no space for anyone to express their feelings about this split. Those discussions should have happened before the ritual. The purpose now is to create formal closure, which allows all of you to part with positive and peaceful feelings.

SUPPLIES

◆ A long silver cord

◆ Scissors

NOTES

◆ When a circle is cast, it's not considered proper to leave without "cutting a gate." Using your athame, start at the floor by your left foot and go straight up, across the top, and down on the right side, so that you've made the shape of a door. Seal the gate with three slashes in the shape of a big Z—one slash for casting with the sword/athame/wand, one for cleansing with saltwater, and one for charging with incense. The three slashes quickly recast that section of the circle.

STEPS

1. Cast the circle (page 7).

2. After cakes and wine, ask the Lady and Lord to bless the work you are about to do with love and with gentleness. Ask Them to continue to bless your coven as it changes.

3. One person ties the cord around her own left wrist and hands the cord to the left. Each person ties their wrist and hands the cord left, returning it, finally, to the person who started, so that everyone, including the departing member, is bound.

4. One person speaks:

   "We are [group name]. We are, and have been, bound together, through joys and sorrows, through the love of the Gods.
   Change is a part of life. As summer yields to fall, and fall to winter, and winter becomes spring, so [group name] enters a new season.
   We are bound together, but the shape of this binding will change."

5. With the scissors, cut the knot that binds the departing person to the rest of you. The person steps back. Take the severed ends and retie them, so that the rest of the group is still interconnected.

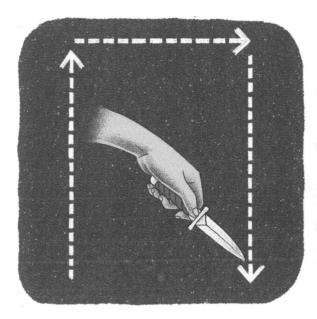

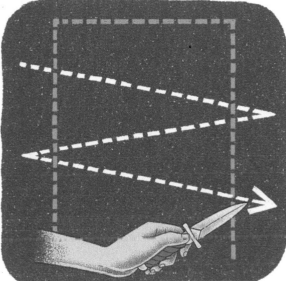

CUTTING THE GATE   **SEALING THE GATE**

◆ If you have a coven token (see "Blessing a New Group," page 58), all of you should wear it.

6. The departing person says:

   "*I leave [group name] behind.*"
   He takes off his coven token and leaves it on the altar.

7. All remaining coven members say:

   "*Go in peace.*"

8. The departing person now cuts a gate and leaves the circle, then leaves the premises entirely, without further goodbyes.

9. Close the circle (page 8) only after the departing member is gone.

Non-Coven Groups and Pairs

You can share magic with people who aren't witches,
and this can be wonderfully empowering as well.

Cohabitation Harmony

Not everyone who is interested in energy, or even magic, identifies as a witch
or wants to be part of a coven. Sometimes, like-minded people are roommates
but not covenmates. The idea of this rite is to send energy toward a harmonious
living situation without necessarily casting a circle, so that your different paths
and beliefs are all respected. Discuss everything that will be done in advance,
and allow anyone to make changes—the communication and shared responsi-
bility are part of the magic!

   This list you generate for this spell is a great way to open up communication
and set boundaries. Don't go overboard by regulating every moment of behavior. On the other hand, a basic cleaning schedule and things like "no smoking"
and "rent must be paid by the first" are reasonable agreements.

SUPPLIES

- A previously agreed-upon
  list of household chores,
  responsibilities, and rules

- Drums or percussion
  instruments (enough
  for everyone)

- Everyone's house keys

- Candles and incense for
  atmosphere (optional)

NOTES

- *"So mote it be"* is not
  necessarily a comfortable
  phrase for people who are
  not witches. Variations
  include *"So say we all,"*
  "So be it," *"Hear, hear,"*
  "Make it so," and *"Amen."*

STEPS

1. Begin with deep breathing and perhaps saying "*Om*" or toning together—whatever you're all comfortable with.

2. Say: "*We are here to send positive energy into our household, so that being roommates will be peaceful, happy, and fulfilling for all of us.*"

3. Begin reading the agreements list out loud. Pass the list person to person so that everyone reads a sentence or two.

4. Everyone says: "*So say we all!*"

5. Using the instruments, raise power through percussion while chanting, "*Bless our household.*"

6. Send all the energy into the keys.

7. One at a time, everyone takes their energized keys and says: "*Our household is blessed.*"

8. Declare the work complete.

Loving Each Other: A Magical Date

This is meant for two people who are both magical, to nurture and grow their love by sharing their energy. Sex magic is as old as magic itself. It's a vital expression of the life force, but it's not the only couple energy. Here we blend sexual Fire with the other elements.

SUPPLIES

- Sage bundle or incense

- Whiskey or other spirit

- A poem or piece of writing—one selected by each of you

- Water

- A picnic meal

NOTES

- For a heterosexual couple, it's traditional for the woman to consecrate or bless the man first.

- If you don't drink, use a red candle for the fire blessing.

- You can spend a full day at this, or an evening or afternoon. The opening declaration in step 1 should reflect the appropriate time period ("today," "tonight," etc.).

- You are using an embrace instead of saying "So mote it be."

STEPS

1. Read together:

   "Today we empower our love. By the Gods, by the Elements, by all powers, let magic fill our relationship." Embrace.

2. Use the sage or incense to cense each other, and say:

   "By the power of Air, this relationship is blessed with intelligence, thoughtfulness, and imagination." Embrace.

3. Each read your selected piece to the other. Reading is of Air, and this seals the consecration of Air.

4. Toast each other with the spirit (or consecrate by flame), and say:

   "By the power of Fire, this relationship is blessed with passion, life force, and will." Embrace.

5. Now make love. Sex is of Fire, and this seals the consecration of Fire.

6. Sprinkle each other with water, and say:

   "By the power of Water, this relationship is blessed with love, intuition, and dreams." Embrace.

7. Drink the water together to seal the consecration of Water.

8. Take your picnic outside. Lift the bread to your partner, and say:

    "By the power of Earth, this relationship is blessed with commitment, stability, and domesticity." Embrace. Eat the meal. Eating is of Earth, and this seals the consecration of Earth.

9. After you finish eating, walk in nature. Find a spot that feels sacred to you both. With your hands on the earth, say:

    "Lady of Nature, bless this relationship." Embrace.

10. Find a tree that you can hug and hold hands around it. With the tree between you, say:

    "Lord of the Wild Woods, bless this relationship." Embrace.

11. Say:

    "We have been blessed by Air, Fire, Water, and Earth, by the Lady and the Lord. Our relationship is truly consecrated." Embrace.

Finding Love for Each Other: A Magical Trade

Sometimes when we're doing magic for ourselves, we get blocked. This spell is a trade—you and another witch cast love spells for each other, to release blocks either or both of you have. By doing this trade, you can let go of your own desire for love, knowing it's in good hands. You can just focus on magic on behalf of another.

SUPPLIES

- Your friend's "What Do I Want?" list (page 33)

- A red candle, dressed (page 13)

- Your magic pen

- Two pieces of paper

- Pink ribbon

- A red rose

NOTES

- This assumes that each of you has done the "What Do I Want?" spell in advance, or developed a list without the spell.

- Instead of the spell below, you can do a variation on "Bring the Person of My Dreams" spell (page 32). You'd use an additional candle for your friend instead of sitting in the center of the candles.

STEPS

1. Prior to doing any magic, sit with each other and read each other your lists. Get descriptive. Ask questions. Make sure you both know what the other wants and that you're able to visualize the other's ideal partner. Your friend is going to do a spell for you, and you will do a spell for your friend.

2. Begin the ritual by lighting the candle and meditating on your friend.

3. Draw a picture, stick figure, or symbol representing your friend's ideal lover.

4. Write your friend's list directly over the picture.

5. On the second sheet, draw your friend. Over the picture, write the positive qualities your friend has; things you think would be on someone else's list.

6. Concentrating on these two people, place the sheets so that they face each other and touch.

7. Wrap the sheets around the rose stem.

- Steps 1 and 2 should take place on a separate occasion from the rest of the spell.

8. Holding the sheets, gaze at the candle, seeing your friend happily partnered.

9. Let the candle burn out fully. The sheets can be buried, dropped in free-flowing water, or hidden away until the goal is achieved.

Spells of Ending

E ndings are as much a part of life as beginnings. No matter how we pray for stability, everything changes. Endings open the way for the next beginning, after all, and death is what brings rebirth.

In this chapter, we look at facing unwanted endings in a positive way, as well as fostering much-needed endings through our magic. Remember, "positive" doesn't mean "put on a happy face." We can cry, be sad, and still create a positive outcome. These spells will help get you there.

Facing Unwanted Endings

These are spells and rites for saying goodbye
even when we wish we didn't have to.

Bless the Departed Soul

There is no greater ending, no harder loss, than death itself. Most of us, sooner or later, face a death where, as witches, our rites are not welcome at the funeral, wake, or shiva call. We have to do these separately, on our own, and that can make it harder. This rite eases the passage for the deceased as well as for you, the mourner.

SUPPLIES

- A white candle
- A black candle, dressed (page 13—dress down and widdershins for departure)
- A headscarf or hood
- A picture of the deceased
- A dish of salt
- A symbol or statuette of the Horned God of Death (optional)

NOTES

- This rite can be done as soon as you hear about the death, regardless of moon or planetary phase.

- A cast circle is optional. You might find it comforting to do a full ritual, or you might find it overwhelming, because you're shocked or upset. Every situation is different.

STEPS

1. If you have cast a circle, invoke the Horned God of Death, and do these steps after cakes and wine (page 8).

2. Begin with the white candle already lit.

3. Light the black candle and put out the white candle. Put on your head covering. (You can bow to the statue of the Horned One here.) Say:

   "Death has come. The light of [name] has gone out on this Earth."

4. Take the black candle to each quarter in turn, and say:

   "Guardians of the East/South/West/North, look upon the soul of [name] as they cross the veil. Guard them and protect them on their journey. Look kindly upon them."

   Make a final, silent, stop at the East, before returning the candle to the altar.

5. Place the candle and the picture next to each other so you can look at both together. Say:

   "[Name], it's time for me to say goodbye to you. May your journey be blessed. May you be reborn to a happy life. May we meet again. Blessed be."

6. Take a pinch of salt and put it on the flame of the black candle so that it snuffs the flame.

7. Remove your hood and relight the white candle. Say:

   "In rebirth there is joy. In time, I will feel this and know this. Today I mourn. My sorrow will be transformed. I trust this to be true. So mote it be."

8. Close the circle (page 8) if it was cast.

Time to Say Goodbye

This is a spell for saying goodbye when a door has closed. It might not be sad, but it's final. Examples of this situation: Your adult child has moved out, your ex has gotten married, or your best friend has transitioned (in this case, you're saying goodbye to your perception of their prior gender identity to support and greet your friend in their affirmed identity).

SUPPLIES

♦ Three gray or black votive candles, dressed (page 13)

♦ Six gold or yellow taper candles, dressed

NOTES

♦ The numbers and colors correspond to appropriate planetary energies.

♦ Your incense should be strong and purifying, like frankincense.

STEPS

1. Arrange the candles in three triangles, as illustrated.

2. Cast the circle (page 7).

3. After cakes and wine, begin describing the "old," the thing you're saying goodbye to. Talk about it, invoke it, sing a song about it. Meanwhile, go around widdershins and light the gray candles.

4. Take some deep, cleansing breaths. Say "*Om*" or tone, moving energy through your body head to toe and back again. Breathe deeper and hotter, until you feel full of energy.

5. Moving deosil, begin describing the new, the thing you're making room for, as you light the gold candles. Sing a song of welcome.

6. After you close the circle, you can move all nine candles to someplace safe where you can see them as they burn down. Votives last about half as long as tapers, so the "old" will be gone while the "new" continues to burn. You can meditate on this as you see the candles.

Divorce Blessing

When marriage ends, it can be ugly, but it doesn't have to be. Especially if you have children together, you will stay connected, and maximizing the positive will be good for you and for the kids.

It's important, too, to understand that when you gave marriage vows, you were magically bound by them. Unwinding that binding, then, heals the wound caused by a broken vow.

This divorce blessing is a retaking of your wedding vows, in a way that reinterprets them for the new relationship you will have. It is a reversal of marriage.

SUPPLIES

◆ A cord, prepared with as many knots as there are vows

NOTES

◆ Ideally this should be done by both partners. If necessary, do it alone, invoking your patron Gods and asking them to listen.

STEPS

1. Get your original marriage vows and work on rewriting them. As an example, here are the wedding vows from the *Book of Common Prayer*, with a potential rewrite.

   Breaking it up into lines as shown is important, since each line will be a knot.

2. Now you're ready for the rite, which should be performed on a Saturday during a waning moon. Ideally, a place meaningful to the two of you should be used for this rite, and both divorcing partners should be present.

3. Do whatever invocations were done at your wedding. If you asked God to bless your union, ask God to be present now.

4. Each of you hold the cord. Recite the first Divorce Vow, and as you do so, untie the first knot.

5. When the cord has no knots left, say, "*So mote it be.*" Bury the cord.

Wedding Vow	Divorce Vow
Will you have this man to be your husband;	*You will no longer be my spouse, but you will always be my friend.*
to live together in the covenant of marriage?	*We will no longer live together, but we remain in covenant, as co-parents.*
Will you love him, comfort him, honor and keep him,	*I will always love you, and honor you, knowing the person you are,*
in sickness and in health; and,	*In sickness and in health.*
forsaking all others,	*I will welcome the new people in your life,*
be faithful to him	*As a faithful friend,*
as long as you both shall live?	*As long as we both do live.*

Affirmations to Ease a Broken Heart

A broken heart can literally sicken you. It is as physical as it is emotional. It's equally important to say goodbye, and to work affirmatively to heal.

SUPPLIES

- Paper and pen to write your affirmations
- Adhesive tape to hang them

NOTES

- The rules of affirmations are: **present tense, affirmative, positive,** and **real**. If you say *"I want to be happy,"* you are affirming that you *want* to be happy. Instead say, *"I am happy." "Am"* is the present tense.

- Don't negate. Say *"I am happy,"* not *"I am not depressed."* The deep mind throws away the extra negating word, and hears, *"I am ~~not~~ depressed."*

STEPS

1. Write one to three affirmations that are pertinent and personal for you.

   Examples:
   My heart is whole. I am healed and ready for the next step in life.
   Heartache is in the past. Today I am at peace.
   I am at peace and open to love.
   My life is full of love.

2. Hang the affirmation(s) by your mirror.

3. Repeat each affirmation 12 times while looking in the mirror. Do this daily for at least 28 days—a full moon cycle.

Necessary Endings

There are times in life when we need things to end,
and must work toward making that happen.

Releasing Rage

Rage can be cleansing. If we were abused, rage at our abusers is righteous and strong. It can drive away depression and self-loathing. Eventually, though, it has to yield to positivity, or it poisons us. This spell names the rage and burns it up so that we can move on. This can be a *great* group ritual with like-minded others.

SUPPLIES

- Materials for building and putting out a fire (kindling, starter fluid, wood, a bucket, and a fire extinguisher)
- A utility knife
- A permanent marker
- Your athame or wand
- A drum or rattle

STEPS

1. Find a private outdoor location and build a fire. Set a number of smaller pieces of wood aside.

2. Think about your rage. Smooth a piece of wood with your utility knife so there's a writable surface. Write your rage in marker, for example, "*I hate my father*," or "*rape*." Do not write people's names—you are destroying rage, not human beings. Use as many pieces of wood as needed in order to fully express yourself.

3. One piece at a time, read the rage out loud. Scream and shout. For example, "*Screw you, rape!*"

4. Throw that rage on the fire and tell it to burn. Repeat this for each piece of wood.

5. Point your athame or wand at the fire, screaming, "*Burn away, rage! Burn away, rage!*"

6. Drum or rattle, raising and sending power into this release.

7. Safely douse the fire before leaving.

Spell to Quit Smoking

For this spell, it's important to have a specific reason for *why* you're quitting. People often say things like "I should" or "It's not good for me," but those aren't explicitly personal reasons. Here are some I experienced: I was tired of having to stop for cigarettes no matter where I was going; I was afraid it would cause wrinkles; it made the pain of Raynaud's disease worse. You can do this spell and still use whatever medical aids you need, such as nicotine patches, Wellbutrin, or other chosen therapies—the magic will bolster your quitting efforts.

This spell asks that you give yourself a gift. Choose something rewarding and positive, something that won't make you feel bad. Replacing cigarettes with chocolate, for example, can create negative feelings around food or weight. I chose nice pens—I love them, and they feel good in my hand the way cigarettes did.

SUPPLIES

◆ Your last pack of cigarettes

◆ A present to yourself, gift-wrapped

NOTES

◆ Perform this spell outdoors during a waning moon.

STEPS

1. Meditate on what it feels like to smoke.

2. Hold your cigarettes and speak to them. Tell them why you love them: *"You've been there for me when I've been afraid. You've calmed me."* Pour out all the love you've lavished on cigarettes.

3. Now begin to say goodbye. Use your clear, detailed reasons, and specifically state that you are saying goodbye and you are done. Thank your cigarettes for what they've given to you.

4. When you're ready, crumble the cigarettes into bits, and say *"Thank you, goodbye"* as you do so. The paper and tobacco can be left to the Earth. Filters should be thrown into the garbage.

5. Get up and walk away. Find a different spot, a few feet or a long walk away.

6. Say, *"As I let go of the old, wonderful new things come in."* Unwrap your gift.

Sever the Ties

Sage is the purifying and cleansing herb at the heart of this spell. It's especially good at releasing attachments. What you're doing with the sage, though, is not "smudging"—this term is specific to Native American rituals.

SUPPLIES

- A spool of black thread
- Your athame or another knife
- A sage bundle

NOTES

- Some people *never* use the athame for cutting; you can make an exception for this spell, or you can use two knives: the athame to cut energy, and another knife to cut the thread. Some people have a ritual "white-handled knife" for cutting.

- Perform this spell skyclad, during a waning moon, in a room with a mirror (preferably full-length).

STEPS

1. Think about the attachment you're releasing. (If it doesn't come *flooding* into your mind, it's probably not worth doing this spell!) Let the thoughts find locations in your body: *This* part is in my hands, *this* part is in my throat. Begin tying black thread around each area.

2. Look in the mirror. See all the threads. Notice that they're ugly and that you don't want them.

3. Using your athame or white-handled knife, start cutting the threads away. As you do so, say *"I cut this attachment"* each time. If you can be more specific, do so. Maybe one thread is *"his grip"* and another is *"his voice."* Keep the *"I cut"* part of the phrase.

4. Look in the mirror again. See yourself freed. See how much better you look without all those ugly black threads.

5. With your athame, cut all around your body, severing all invisible attachments. Get the top of your head, the soles of your feet, every inch of you, back and front. You're cutting without touching the skin, about a half-inch from your body, close enough so that it's inside your "etheric body."

6. Now light the sage bundle and trace your body in the same way with the smoke, and say *"I am free"* over and over.

7. Get dressed and take the loose threads outside. Bury them, and say *"You are dead and buried! So mote it be!"* Make sure you bury them *off* your property. Do not keep these threads on land you own or rent, or that is "yours" in any way.

8. Repeat the sage bundle clearing (step 6) every day until the new moon.

Break a Bad Habit

Addictions are one thing (see "Spell to Quit Smoking," page 78), but they aren't the limit of bad habits. Whether you're a procrastinator, a hoarder, or a nail-biter, breaking bad habits can be a struggle.

This is an ancient magical technique and works by moving the energy gradually, which is easier than changing cold turkey.

SUPPLIES

- A long taper candle, dressed (page 13)

- Ten straight pins or black-headed pins

- Rattles or other instruments (optional)

NOTES

- The color of the candle depends on the habit you're trying to break. If you can't come up with an appropriate color, white always works.

- Begin two days after the full moon.

STEPS

1. Prepare the candle by sticking the pins into it horizontally, at regular intervals.

2. Cast the circle (page 7).

3. After cakes and wine, ask the Gods you worship to help you break this habit.

4. Light the candle, and say: *"As this candle burns away, so my [habit] burns away and is gone."*

5. Raise power in a way that relates to the work: If your habit is laziness, get up and dance. If your habit is procrastination, use quick movements (perhaps with a rattle or other instrument). Or use a chant with words that create the positive alternative to this habit you need.

6. Send your power into the candle. Say again, *"Burn away, [habit], burn away!"*

7. Let the candle burn until the first pin falls. You can close the circle before that happens, but make sure the candle is where you're paying attention to it. Snuff the candle when the pin falls.

   For the next eight nights, light the candle and repeat, *"As this candle burns away, so my [habit] burns away and is gone."* Let the candle burn until the next pin falls. You don't have to gaze at the candle the entire time, but make sure you're paying attention so that you snuff it when the pin falls.

8. On the 10th night, when there are no more pins, let the candle burn all the way down.

9. Dispose of the pins in free-running water (like a stream) or, if necessary, in the garbage.

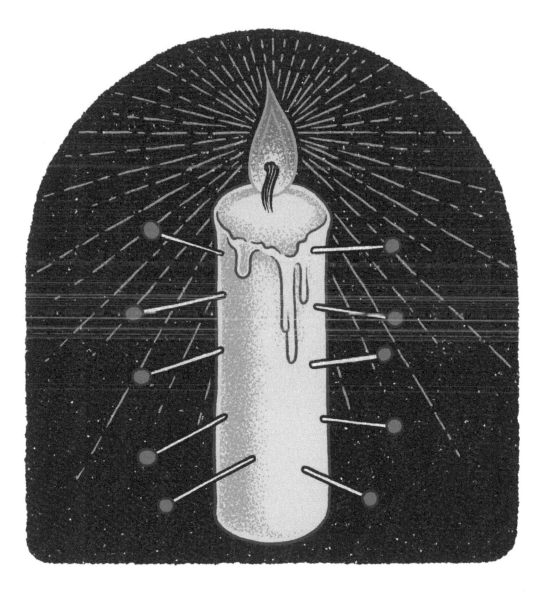

Sweep Away an Enemy

Banish your enemies positively. This spell gets them out of your life without causing harm.

SUPPLIES

◆ A candle, dressed (yellow, silver, or gray—the colors of the planet Mercury) (page 13)

◆ A broom

NOTES

◆ Perform this spell on a Wednesday during a waning moon.

STEPS

1. Cast the circle (page 7).

2. After cakes and wine, ask the Gods you worship to send your enemy far from you, to someplace she'll be happy. Emphasize that your enemy will be better off, more successful, more fulfilled, in the new place.

3. Light the candle, stating your intention:

   "[Name] will be gone from my life.
   [Name] will be far from here."
   Repeat this several times, building power.

4. When you feel your power is at its peak, pick up your broom and sweep, widdershins, three times around the perimeter of the circle, starting and ending in the East. As you sweep, visualize your enemy being swept away, and say:

   "[Name] is swept away
   [Name] I never see
   As is my will
   So mote it be!"
   Repeat this over and over as you sweep. End with *"So mote it be!"*

5. Snuff the candle.

6. Close the circle (page 8).

Spells to Heal and Soothe

As a witch, the majority of my work is healing. Healing spells can be psychological or physical, for ourselves or others. Self-healing when you're physically sick is hard, because you'll lack the energy needed for magic; it's best to confine your self-healing to the emotional and psychological.

Healing magic is not a substitute for medical treatment; it's "companion therapy." Avoiding the doctor says you're not really committed to recovery, and that disempowers magic.

This chapter starts with self-help spells, followed by a section on elemental work in healing, and finally, a general healing section.

Self-Help and Emotional Work

These spells are written as self-help, but they can be
done for yourself or for another. They're all within
the area of psychological, emotional, and mental work.

Finding a Path: A Labyrinth Spell

This spell uses the ancient labyrinth to find out where you're going in life. There
are any number of ways to acquire a labyrinth, including carving, affixing beads
to a piece of wood, or even printing out a picture. Labyrinths can be stitched,
sculpted, etched, or painted; homemade or purchased.

An alternative, using your full body, is to walk a labyrinth. I've seen these set
up in yards and fields, marked with stones or tea lights for temporary rites, or
planted for permanent ritual sites. You walk to the center, meditate there, and
walk back out. It's a beautiful group rite as well.

SUPPLIES

- A labyrinth, at least six
  inches square, and a stylus
  (any piece of wood with a
  tapered end)

- A blue candle, dressed
  (page 13)

STEPS

1. Cast the circle (page 7).

2. After cakes and wine, ask the Gods you worship to help
   you find a path. Let Them know you'll be working to discover which way you should go, and ask Their help.

3. Clear your mind, light the candle, and ask your question
   out loud.

4. Begin tracing the labyrinth with the stylus. Follow the
   path slowly and deliberately to the center and out again.
   Do this over and over. It will begin to feel trance-like.
   Keep going as long as feels right. End with *So mote it be.*

5. Close the circle (page 8), confident that the way will soon
   be clear. Let the candle burn all the way out.

Too Many Options: A Spell to Choose

Sometimes abundance is a problem, whether it's too many college acceptances, too many lovers to fit your schedule, or too many ideas of what to write next.

SUPPLIES

◆ Your athame or wand

◆ As many pennies as you have options, in a small dish

STEPS

1. Centered and grounded, concentrate on your concern. Visualize clearly the choice you must make.

2. Plunge your athame or wand into the dish of pennies. As you send power, recite:

> *"Too much! Too many!*
> *I choose just one shiny penny.*
> *I choose the penny meant for me.*
> *To help me shape my destiny."*

3. Put the pennies into your pocket and go out for a walk, ideally in nature. Every now and then, take a penny, recite your rhyme, and toss the penny far away.

4. When there's only one penny left in your pocket, go home.

5. Sleep with the penny under your pillow every night until your choice is made.

Attitude Adjustment

This spell addresses the negativity we sometimes pile on ourselves. If negative thoughts continue to plague you, combine this spell with basic shielding (page 105).

This is a process of self-discovery. If positive traits are more difficult for you than negative ones (as they are for most of us), ask yourself why that is—but don't give up! The positive traits are there. If you get truly stuck, and it becomes too painful to proceed, please see the note at the end of the book (page 178).

Just as healing spells are not a substitute for medical help, self-help spells are not a substitute for therapy or antidepressants. Self-care means accessing the full range of options available to you.

SUPPLIES

◆ Magic pen and paper

STEPS

1. Draw a line down the center of the page, and on the left side of the line, write a list of all the negative things about yourself. Write every thought that plagues you about yourself. Don't hold back.

2. Cast a circle (page 7).

3. After cakes and wine, ask the Gods you worship to assist you in understanding how good and worthy you are.

4. On the right side of the line, write only positive traits. The rule is that you *must* have as many positive traits as negative ones.

5. Read your positive list out loud. Know that the Gods notice, and celebrate, your positive traits.

6. Say:

> *"These positive traits are who I am.*
> *I banish negative thinking.*
> *I am [read one or more positive traits]!*
> *I banish negative thinking.*
> *I am [read one or more additional positive traits]!*
> *I banish negative thinking.*
> *I am [read one or more additional positive traits]!*
> *I banish negative thinking.*
> *So mote it be!"*

   Continue this chant for as long as you want, with any or all traits, repeating traits if you like.

7. Thank the Gods and pour an additional offering. Close the circle (page 8).

8. Carry your list with you. When you find yourself reverting to negative thoughts, choose a positive trait from your list and tell yourself *"I am [trait]."*

Pleasant Dreams: An Anti-Nightmare Mojo Bag

If you've been having nightmares, this spell combines a self-blessing with a sleep sachet to drive them away.

The "mojo bag" is a common technique in magic. It is made from a store-bought or homemade bag or cloth square (perhaps of a meaningful color), then filled with herbs, crystals, or other objects, and marked with sigils or symbols.

SUPPLIES

♦ A small square of cloth and a silver ribbon to tie it up, or a small cloth bag

♦ Silver paint or a silver marker

♦ Cedar shavings or cedar chips

♦ Censer and charcoal

♦ A dish of water

♦ Your wand or athame

♦ Anise seeds, rosemary, and thyme, in a dish

NOTES

♦ The square can be used as a cloth bag by bringing the corners together once the herbs are in it, and tying them with the ribbon.

STEPS

1. Prepare your bag or cloth by inscribing a crescent moon on the outside in silver with paint or marker.

2. Burn the cedar as incense. When it's smoking, cense yourself with it, and say:

   "I bless my dreams by Air and Fire."

3. Anoint your third eye with water, and say:

   "I bless my dreams by Water."

4. With your wand or athame, send power into the herb mixture, and say:

   "I bless my dreams by herbs of Earth."

5. Tie the herbs into the bag or bundle and sleep with it under your pillow.

Elemental Healing

The four elements are a crucial part of smart, targeted healing spells. Following are four examples of elemental healing spells, with some extra information on how to use Air, Fire, Water, and Earth in all your work.

Each of the four spells is written as self-healing, but can be modified to heal others, locally or remotely (see "Method for Distant Healing," page 96). Each can also be used as an elementally targeted component of a broader healing ritual.

Water My Blood

Water is considered the element of healers. Diseases related to the body's waters—blood and lymphatic fluid—are Water. Amniotic fluid is also Water, so Water can help pregnancy. Psychologically, Water rules depression, mood swings, and sleep disorders. Using wine, sticky-floral jasmine, or rose scents, and fruits like apple and peach can all bring Water to a spell.

To use Water in a cast circle, bring shells, invoke deities of the sea, and incorporate drinking and wine into your spell. Work this spell outdoors or in a bath so you can pour freely.

SUPPLIES

- Water in a beautiful goblet

- Seashells

NOTES

- Water is spontaneous, so make up your words on the spot.

STEPS

1. Describe your purpose, invoking Water's aid in healing.

2. Speak to the water in the goblet, touching it, allowing yourself to be absorbed by it.

3. Sing a freeform song (words are optional) that includes the following idea (if not these exact words): "*Water, heal me.*"

4. Pour the water over yourself, touching parts of you that need healing.

5. End with "*So mote it be.*"

Air My Breath

In physical healing, Air is used for breathing. In psychological and emotional healing, Air is inspiration and logic. Use Air, such as this spell, to heal the lungs and clear the mind.

Writing spells are also Air spells, since language is Air. For healing, though, I prefer to physically feel air move.

To use Air in a cast circle, you'd add extra Air beyond the balanced four elements on your altar, for example, by adding lavender to the incense after the circle is cast, or by using a hand fan.

SUPPLIES

◆ Feathers

◆ A hand fan

◆ An Air incense, such as lavender, sage, lemongrass, or meadowsweet

NOTES

◆ The feathers serve primarily as decoration, to remind you of Air. Surround your working area with them. They also blow around delightfully when you use the fan, although some people may be bothered by the mess.

◆ This can easily be done outdoors, using the open air to add to the spell.

◆ Because Air *is* language, stating everything out loud is important.

STEPS

1. State your purpose out loud, such as *"I invoke Air, the element of mind, to heal the suffering caused by my executive function disorder."*

2. Light your incense, breathe it in deeply, and say: *"Air, I bring you in."*

3. Fan yourself, head to toe, and say:

   "Air, heal me."

4. End with *"So mote it be."*

Fire My Spirit

Fire heals neurological and autoimmune issues, and rules energy and libido. It is powerful for raising the life force, but should not be used on people in very delicate health, who cannot handle being "blasted" with energy. Generally, such people need Water.

Different magical systems ascribe Fire to the wand and Air to the athame, or vice versa. Other things that bring Fire to a spell are hot spices and spicy foods (like jalapeños), amber, and tiger's eye.

To use Fire in a cast circle, add extra Fire beyond the balanced four elements on your altar, by bringing extra candles, using Fire tools, or adding a Fire incense such as basil or rosemary.

SUPPLIES

- A large red candle or group of candles

- Your athame or wand

STEPS

1. Light the candle(s) and gaze into the flame, allowing yourself to enter Fire.

2. Bring the Fire toward you, mentally or physically, and say: "*I invoke Fire.*" Hold it near whatever part of you needs healing, feeling the heat.

3. Move the feeling of heat throughout your body. Regardless of the medical condition, make sure to move the heat to your groin, as arousal awakens the body's Fire.

4. Hold your athame or wand, point it toward the Fire, and say: "*Fire, heal me!*"

5. Wave your hands over the flame, bringing it toward your body, repeating: "*Fire, heal me!*" As you do so, dance and sway as you feel moved.

6. End with "*So mote it be.*"

Earth My Body

Because Earth rules the physical body, it is vital in healing. Earth corresponds to muscle, bone, tissue, and most organs. It is related to appetite—both the loss of appetite and obesity. Earth strengthens, stabilizes, and grounds. It can help with PTSD, rooting the sufferer in the here and now, though it is not a replacement for medical treatments and therapies.

Things that bring Earth to a spell include salt, eating (bread, specifically), deep bass drumming, milk, and planting. To use Earth in a cast circle, add stones to the altar, invoke the Earth Mother, and incorporate eating or the planting of seeds into your spell.

SUPPLIES

◆ Stones

◆ Salt in a dish

◆ A bowl of potting soil

◆ A drum (optional)

NOTES

◆ Surround your working area (indoors or out) with stones.

STEPS

1. Spend additional time—above and beyond your normal preparations—in grounding before you begin.

2. Call upon Mother Earth for help in your work.

3. Put a grain of salt on your tongue.

4. Using slow, rhythmic speech, say: *"I invoke the element of Earth."* You can stomp your feet with each syllable, like: *"I! In! Voke! The! El! E! Ment! Of! Earth!"*

5. Finding a rhythm with your feet and/or drum, shift to *"Earth! Heal! Me!"* Try drumming on your body, slapping your legs, belly, chest, or arms.

6. At the peak, plunge your hands deep into the potting soil, and say: *"So mote it be."*

General Healing

These are general healing spells for a variety of needs. Combine them with the elemental spells to fine-tune your work.

Spell for Cancer

When someone we love has cancer, it can be terrifying, and we can feel real despair. One of the joys of witchcraft is the ability to do something; to fight back.

SUPPLIES

♦ A poppet of the patient (page 98) with the location of the cancer marked

NOTES

♦ Use your wand if you don't have an athame, but an athame adds the idea of "cutting" away the cancer.

♦ Cancer spells are unusual among healing spells, in that they are generally waning moon spells. You are *shrinking* the tumor, *diminishing* or *destroying* the metastasis.

STEPS

1. Cast the circle (page 7).

2. After cakes and wine, consecrate the poppet by the four elements, and by the Gods, as in "Method for Distant Healing" (page 96).

3. Gaze at your poppet, *seeing* the person you are healing. *Know* that this is the person you are healing.

4. Raise power with rhythm, song, movement, or concentration.

5. As you send power with your athame into the poppet, see the person completely well. Imagine them doing something really fun, something they love, with a joyful expression. Concentrate on that image as you pour energy into the poppet.

6. End by saying "*So mote it be!*"

7. Close the circle (page 8).

Method for Distant Healing

Laying on of hands is powerful, but you can also send your magic elsewhere. This technique works for a variety of spells and can be modified to heal any sort of illness or injury.

From the beginning of Wicca, it has been said that the magic circle is "between the worlds." Since you are not in *this* world, you are not miles and miles away from anything or anyone else in this world. Distant healing uses this idea.

SUPPLIES

- A photograph of the person being healed

- Any additional personal item connected to that person, such as a gift they gave you, something in their handwriting, etc. (optional)

NOTES

- Modify the circle casting to say: "*This is a circle between the worlds, a place that is not a place, sacred, protected, a source of power. Here, all things are possible. So mote it be!*" This phrasing emphasizes the otherworldly nature of the circle that you'll use to do your magic.

- A poppet (page 98) could be used instead of a photograph.

STEPS

1. Cast the circle (page 7), modified as in the note.

2. After cakes and wine, pass the photo (and other item if you have it) through the incense smoke, and say:

   "*By Air and Fire, this is [Name].*
   [Name] is here in this circle.
   This is [Name] and [Name] is here!"

3. Now wet the photo/item with saltwater. You can avoid damaging the photo if need be, but make sure you get all of it—top and bottom, front and back. Say:

   "*By Water and Earth, this is [Name].*
   [Name] is here in this circle.
   This is [Name] and [Name] is here!"

4. Hold the photo up to the Gods you worship, and say:

   "*Lady and Lord, see that this is [Name].*
   See that [Name] is here.
   Beloved Gods, lend your aid as I heal [Name] in this circle.
   So mote it be!"

5. From this point, you can do any healing you choose. You can do elemental healing as on the previous pages, raise a cone (page 57) if you're in a group, or work a spell you have created. "Spell for Cancer" (page 95), "Healing a Sick Child" (page 97), or "What's Wrong? A Diagnosis Spell" (page 100) can all be done distantly with this technique.

Healing a Sick Child

When a child is sick, it's helpful to connect to them in a childlike manner, in order for the energy to reach them. Singing is one way to do that.

SUPPLIES

- A poppet (page 98), photo, or toy, representing the child

NOTES

- I prefer not to use a wand or athame with a child, because I am treating them as if they were in my arms, and I am gently using my hands.

- I've used this spell to great effect. Similarly, I've done pet healing using "meows."

STEPS

1. Cast the circle (page 7).

2. After cakes and wine, consecrate the poppet by the four elements, and by the Gods, as in "Method for Distant Healing" (page 96).

3. Begin singing nursery rhymes or kids' songs. You are raising power with song, but you are doing it in a particularly childlike manner. I especially like ones that come with movement, such as:

   - Six Little Ducks

   - Head, Shoulders, Knees, and Toes

   - If You're Happy and You Know It

   - The Itsy-Bitsy Spider

4. At the point where you're peaking, send the energy with your hands, through the symbol (poppet, photo, toy) directly to the child.

5. Close the circle (page 8).

How to Make a Poppet

A poppet is an ancient magical object, cross-cultural and far older than Wicca. Whether it is called a "voodoo doll" or a corn husk dolly, people all over the world have used little dolls to represent people and animals in their magic. Poppets can be used for love, fertility, protection, healing, and more. There are many other ways to make poppets besides this one, such as with corn husks, professional doll-making supplies, or molded wax.

SUPPLIES

- 2 pieces of cloth
- Chalk to mark the fabric
- Scissors
- Embroidery thread, fabric paint, or permanent marker for decoration
- Needle and thread for sewing the cloth
- Cotton/cotton balls to stuff the poppet
- Herbs, crystals, and other objects for additional stuffing
- Yarn for hair

NOTES

- Colors of cloth, thread, decorations, and type of stuffing can all be symbolic and specific to the work.

STEPS

1. Draw a simple body outline on one piece of cloth.

2. Hold the two pieces together and cut out the body, so that you have two identical pieces.

3. On one piece, use embroidery, paint, or markers to create a face.

4. Also mark the part of the body being targeted—the location of a tumor, for example, can be marked with an X.

5. Some people always add a heart; some only do so for love magic or cardiac healing.

6. Sew the pieces together, leaving openings in the body and head for stuffing. Be sure to leave an opening on the part of the body being targeted.

7. Stuff the doll with cotton, then add your targeted ingredients: Bay leaves for healing, hawthorn for fertility, amethyst for sobriety, etc. The "special" ingredients should be added to the targeted body part.

8. Sew up the openings.

9. Add yarn for hair.

10. Add additional magical decorations or anything that you feel makes your poppet more like the person it represents. Your poppet is now complete. You'll consecrate it when you do the magic.

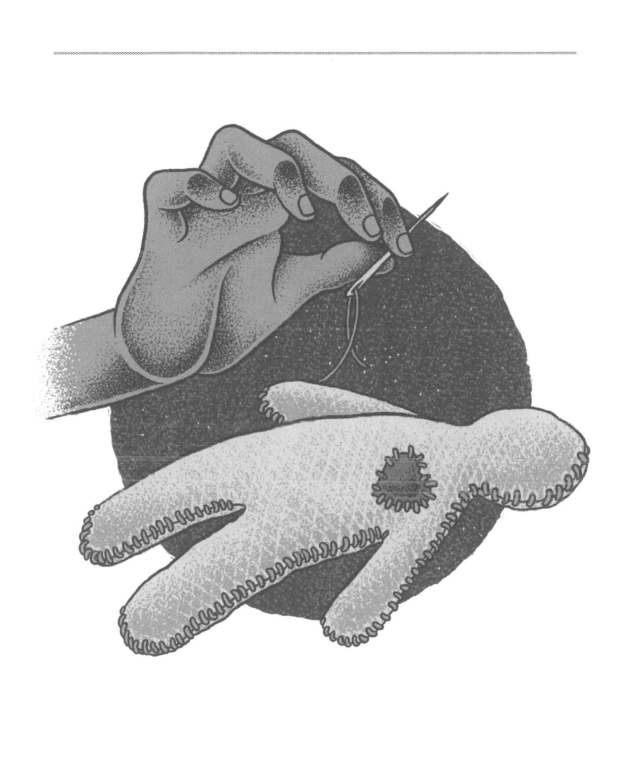

What's Wrong? A Diagnosis Spell

Sometimes you don't care about a diagnosis—you just want to get better. Other times, knowledge is power. When my kid was mysteriously ill, they said they needed Dr. House. There were too young to know that show was just fiction. With magic, we found a doctor who successfully diagnosed and treated my child.

Knowledge and information are Air, so this is an Air spell.

SUPPLIES

- Air incense, such as lavender, sage, lemongrass, or meadowsweet
- A hand fan
- A blindfold

NOTES

- There are different ways to do this spell:
  - In a group, with the patient
  - In a group, without the patient—the person closest to the patient plays the role of the patient
  - Alone—use a poppet as the patient

STEPS

1. Cast the circle (page 7).

2. After cakes and wine, do an additional invocation, for a God or Goddess of healing, such as Asclepius, Bridget, Isis, or Sekhmet.

3. If a poppet is used instead of the patient, use the consecration as in "Method for Distant Healing" (page 96). If a person substitutes for the patient, do the same, but be sure to say they are [Name] for the duration of the spell.

4. Blindfold the patient or surrogate.

5. Chant *"I know, I see, I know, I see"* as you raise power (if a group, raise the cone, page 57). Use your fan to direct power.

6. At peak, pull the blindfold off, shouting: *"I know, I see, so mote it be!"*

7. Close the circle (page 8).

Soothe Me to Sleep

The "Pleasant Dreams" mojo bag (page 90) is to help with nightmares, but if you're not sleeping at all, this tea can help. Keep in mind that insomnia can have medical causes, so speak to a doctor. If your insomnia is due to illness or an anxiety disorder, this spell can work *with* treatment, but isn't meant to shoulder the burden alone. Sleep is Water, so this is a Water spell.

SUPPLIES

- Your athame
- A large goblet or bowl of water
- A kettle, mug, and spoon
- Chamomile and/or valerian
- A tea ball or strainer

NOTES

- You can get the loose herbs, or teas with these herbs, at any health food store.
- Perform the spell shortly before bedtime.

STEPS

1. Consecrate the water with your athame.

2. Pour the water into the kettle, and say:

   "Sacred water, bring sleep to me tonight."

3. While you bring the water to a boil, consecrate the herbs with your athame, and say:

   "Sacred herbs, bring sleep to me tonight."

4. Put the tea in the tea ball or strainer.

5. When the water boils, pour it into your mug.

6. Stir the tea clockwise, singing a lullaby. Sing a favorite from your childhood, or one you've sung to your own child, or one you find soothing. Sing the tea to sleep, turning it into a potion of sleep. Visualize sleep pouring from your song into the mug. Continue for several minutes.

7. Drink the tea, knowing its effects will soon be felt.

CHAPTER 7

Spells of Protection and Courage

In this chapter, we'll be talking about protecting our-selves and others. Often, protection doesn't mean there's anything bad going on: Magical protection is simply the umbrella you carry—it doesn't mean there's anything wrong with rain. Sometimes, though, we use protection against real harm, and it's wonderful to be able to do that.

This chapter starts with self and then home protection, moves on to travel protection, and then dives into special situations calling for special spells.

Self-Protection

Witchcraft begins with protecting yourself. You've surely heard it said that you can't love others until you love yourself. The same is true of protection!

Fast Protection

This quick charm allows you to protect yourself when some unexpected threat appears, whether a snarling dog or your ex-lover.

SUPPLIES

◆ None

NOTES

◆ If you can also put up your shield (page 105) at the same time, all the better.

◆ Memorize the charm and visualization so you can use it at any time.

STEPS

1. Recite the following charm under your breath:

   "Power of the Goddess
   Power of the God
   Cool as a breeze
   Warm as a stove
   Flowing like a stream
   Solid as a stone
   So mote it be!"

2. With each line, visualize an electric blue ring of flame encircling you, so that there is a seven-ring spiral from head to toe.

Essential All-Purpose Shield

As you train yourself to be more sensitive to energies, or become more in touch with your natural sensitivities, shielding allows you to work sanely, happily, and in good health.

Some people use daily shields, some only when they're feeling stressed, drained, or are in a particularly at-risk or overwhelming situation.

There are *many* different shielding techniques. This is the one I use. If you don't find it meets your needs, continue to explore this important topic.

SUPPLIES

- None

NOTES

- This is not a ritual per se, and you won't do full ritual preparations, but always begin by centering and grounding.

- When you first begin using this technique, it will take several minutes. With practice, you'll be shielding in seconds.

STEPS

1. Imagine you're wearing a great pair of polarized sunglasses. Polarization keeps the bad (UV rays) out but lets the good (light that allows you to see) in. Clearly visualize magic polarization: Good gets in, bad stays out.

2. Now imagine those lenses fully surround you. You have a polarized shield everywhere, including over the top of your head and under the soles of your feet. This shield should be about 9 to 12 inches away from your physical body (so that your etheric body is fully inside). Visualize until you are confident that your shield is solid and protective.

3. Imagine something harmful coming toward you, and see it bounce off the shield, unable to reach you.

4. Now visualize someone wonderful coming to hug you. The shield doesn't stop them, and you enjoy the hug.

5. You're now shielded.

Cone of Silence

This spell creates an amulet of mental protection, shielding you from distractions. It surrounds you in stillness and allows for concentration, or just a peaceful interlude.

SUPPLIES

- A gold candle, dressed (page 13)

- A pair of earplugs

- A flat stone, or piece of wood or of metal, to use as the amulet

- Gold paint and a brush, appropriate for painting the material of the amulet

NOTES

- Perform this spell during a waning moon.

- This spell uses gold to remind ourselves that "Silence is golden."

- If possible, it's nice for your amulet to have a hole so you can wear it on a cord or chain.

- You only need a small amount of paint; the package should indicate what you can and cannot paint on.

STEPS

1. Light the candle, and say:

   "This is the power of silence."

2. Put in the earplugs: For the rest of the spell, sound will be muffled or inaudible.

- Create a bind rune (page 36) of silence in advance.

3. Gaze at the candle, concentrating on the power of silence. Feel silence emanating from the candle and filling the space you're working in.

4. When you're ready, paint the bind rune on your amulet. Feel the power of silence flowing through you, from the candle, into the amulet.

5. Continue gazing at the candle while holding your finished amulet, concentrating on the power entering it.

6. Wear or carry the amulet whenever you need silence.

7. You can recharge your amulet from time to time using a new candle.

This bind rune illustration shows "SHH" for silence,
with one H turned sideways to create the central cross.
Either use this example or create your own.

Home Protection

Protecting your home is almost an instinct—it's something
we all want to do. Part of living a magical life is knowing
that you can feel safe; these spells help create
that feeling, and that reality.

A Witch's Bottle

"Witch bottles" or "witches' bottles" are at least four centuries old. They protect
the home by creating a kind of negative double. Whatever means you harm
finds "you" in the form of the physical parts of you that are included in this
spell. The harm then gets entangled and trapped by the knots, confused by the
glass, bound by the metal, and pierced by everything sharp. If available, consider
adding thorns, eggshells, and burrs to your bottle.

SUPPLIES

- A bottle with a tight cork or cap

- Nails and pins (especially bent ones)

- Broken glass and/or mirror

- Pieces of string, knotted multiple times

- Your own nail and/or hair clippings and/or your own bodily fluids (such as urine)

- A red or black candle to seal the cap

STEPS

1. Assemble all your ingredients, concentrating on the idea of binding negativity where it cannot harm you, anyone who lives with you, or your home.

2. Carefully put all the solid materials into the bottle. You can repeat a short charm, like *"Harm be bound away from me"* as you work.

3. Add the liquids and seal the bottle with the cork/cap, still reciting the charm.

NOTES

- Make the bottle on a Tuesday during a waning moon.

- Folklore has the witch's bottle buried upside-down, outside the front door or under the fireplace (presumably placed during construction of the home). You can also place it under the floorboards or, as a last resort, hide it in a remote corner at the lowest point of your home.

- The safe way to get broken glass/mirror is to wrap a whole piece in a thick towel, hit it with a blunt object like a hammer, and then carefully unwrap it.

- Do not store the bodily fluids—get them right before the work.

4. Light the candle and let the wax drip all around the cap to further seal it.

5. Bury the bottle upside down, or hide it under the floor or in a basement corner.

Keeping Something Hidden

There was a time in my life when I got bored with herbs and crystals and runes, so I invented a "secret potion" using items from the hardware store. It's nice to remember that witchcraft can be very modern, and materials like padlocks can be magical.

SUPPLIES

- Several small padlocks, locked

- A jar with a lid

- Vodka

- Your athame or wand

- A chopstick for "invisible writing"

- The object you're hiding

NOTES

- Begin making the potion the day after the full moon. Perform the spell at the new moon (two weeks later).

- You can create a secrecy bind rune (see illustration) for this spell, use Xs, or use another meaningful sigil.

STEPS

1. Start the potion by putting the padlocks in the jar and pouring the vodka over them.

2. With your athame, send power into the potion, repeating:

   "Keep my secret! Lock it away!"

3. Place the potion outside, exposing it to moonlight.

   Once a night, shake it up and repeat the charm:
   "Keep my secret! Lock it away!"

4. On the new moon, bring your potion inside. Dip your chopstick into the potion as if it were a pen dipped in ink, and write your Xs, bind rune, or sigil on your object, concentrating on how hidden and secret it will be.

This bind rune illustration combines Pertho, for secrecy or mystery, with Algiz, for protection. Either use this example or create your own.

Anti-Theft Amulet

In this spell, you'll create an object with a traditional feel and add anti-theft magic. "Hex signs" are a common sight in Pennsylvania Dutch country. They invoke protection, love, and blessing, and are hung on barns and over front doors, using a nail through the center.

SUPPLIES

- A round wooden disk
- Acrylic (waterproof) paints and polyurethane coating

NOTES

- You could do this spell with a store-bought hex sign as well.
- Cast the circle in a waning moon.

STEPS

1. Create the hex sign: First, paint the disk front solid white. Let the white dry, then add a simple design. The rosette shown here is the most common traditional hex sign, and is said to bring good luck.

2. Optionally, add additional symbols for anti-theft, such as an eye to represent watchfulness, crossed spears or swords, or a bind rune (page 36) of your own creation.

The Anti-Theft Hex Sign

CONTINUED ▶

Anti-Theft Amulet (continued)

3. Finish the hex with a coating of polyurethane if you intend to hang it outside. Don't consecrate it until it is fully dry.

4. Cast a circle (page 7).

5. After cakes and wine, ask the Gods you worship to bless the work you are about to do.

6. Consecrate the hex with Fire and Air, then Water and Earth.

7. Gather power through concentration, drumming, chanting, or another method.

8. When you are ready, hold the hex out toward the East and say in a loud, firm voice:

   "Thieves cannot come from the East!"

This hex sign provides an example to bring good luck, success, and happiness.

9. Repeat in the South, West, and North.

10. Hold the hex above your head, and say:

    "Thieves cannot come from above!"

11. Hold the hex to the floor, and say:

    "Thieves cannot come from below!"

12. Hold it close to your body, repeating *"Thieves cannot come!"* faster and faster, until you reach a peak. Then shout: *"So mote it be!"*

13. Close the circle (page 8).

14. Hang the hex over your front door (on the outside).

This hex sign provides an example to
bring goodwill and abundance.

Travel Protection

There are myriad things that can go wrong on the road,
and travel protection is never a bad idea. I use my all-purpose
shield, plus the below extras, on a regular basis.

Parking Spot Safety

I'm a good citizen—I never park in a reserved spot for people with disabilities, and I never block a hydrant. But sometimes I park at 6:40 in a spot that's legal at 7:00, park in a high-crime neighborhood, or engage in other imperfect behavior. This spell applies to all those circumstances and more.

SUPPLIES

◆ Your car mojo bag
(page 116)

NOTES

◆ You should already know how to shield (page 105).

◆ Since you're doing this on the fly, you won't have done any ritual preparations. Take a moment to center and ground before you begin.

STEPS

1. In the car, parked, hold your car mojo bag in both hands.

2. Perform the "Fast Protection" spell (page 104), but instead of visualizing the spiral around your body, see it around the entire car.

3. Step out of the car and lock it. Look at the car and see the blue electric energy surrounding it and protecting it. With your hands, send strength into that energy before walking away.

Stop a Dangerous Driver

Has this ever happened to you? You're driving and you see someone acting absolutely unsafe on the road—weaving in and out, racing, texting, the works. This spell is designed to help curb that dangerous behavior.

SUPPLIES

- Your car mojo bag (page 116)

NOTES

- I assume you're driving while this is happening. Keep one hand on the wheel, and don't fully center and ground, just *concentrate*. You don't want to drive dangerously in order to do this.

STEPS

1. Hold your car mojo bag in one hand.

2. Take a deep breath; focus your energy while keeping your eyes on the road.

3. Visualize Athena, the Goddess of Justice, who carries a helmet, a spear, a shield, and sometimes an owl with her. Or visualize another deity of justice.

4. As you exhale, let go of the mojo bag, point at the driver, and say: *"Justice!"*

5. The Goddess will do what is right about that driver.

Car Mojo Bag

I keep a consecrated mojo bag hanging from my rearview mirror. It protects against any of the things that can happen *in* or *to* a car. I also use it in other travel spells (see page 114).

SUPPLIES

- Cloth, ribbon, and marker for creating a mojo bag (page 90)

- Ingredients for the bag. Choose from the following, selecting a balance of elements and properties:

    - *Fire*: An iron nail (protection), cumin seeds (anti-theft), dill (protection)

    - *Earth*: Coffee (alertness), barley (protection), dried corn (protection), malachite (traveler's protection)

    - *Water*: Marjoram (protection), aloe (protection), willow wood (protection and witchcraft), moonstone (traveler's protection)

    - *Air*: Parsley (protection), mint (travel), anise (protection)

STEPS

1. Cast the circle (page 7).

2. After cakes and wine, ask the Gods you worship to bless the work you are about to do.

3. Have the symbol on the bag in advance. Assemble your ingredients. As you place each in the bag, you can announce its purpose, as in: *"You are for protection."*

4. Consecrate the bag by passing it through the incense smoke and then wetting it with the saltwater, while reciting the following in a firm, powerful voice:

    "Safety from harm.
    I am protected.
    Safety from theft.
    I am protected.
    Safety from attack.
    I am protected.
    Safety from error.
    I am protected.
    Safety from accident.
    I am protected.
    Safety from falling asleep behind the wheel.
    I am protected.
    Safety from hate.
    I am protected.
    Safety from arrest.
    I am protected."

NOTES

- Create this bag during the waxing moon.

- Mars (red) rules machines, Mercury (silver or orange) rules travel, and Jupiter (deep blue) rules luck and long-distance travel. Use whichever symbol feels right, in the color indicated.

- Follow the general instructions for creating a bag as shown in "Pleasant Dreams" (page 90).

5. Now go to each quarter, lift your bag, and say:

> *"Safety from dangers from the East/South/West/North. I am protected."*

6. Return to the East to give a silent acknowledgment, then return to the altar and say:

> *"So mote it be."*

7. Close the circle (page 8).

8. Keep the bag in your car at all times.

Helping Yourself or Others in Special Situations

So far, this chapter has covered the general kind of protection that everyone tends to need in day-to-day life. Sometimes, though, life is far from ordinary. The following spells and techniques cover situations that are less common.

The Courage to Confront

Sometimes, telling the truth can be agonizing. This spell is designed to give you the courage to face a difficult confrontation.

SUPPLIES

♦ Your athame or wand

♦ A dish with a mix of courage-providing herbs: mustard, thyme, black cohosh, sweet pea

NOTES

♦ The first two herbs are readily available in the supermarket.

♦ If sweet pea cannot be found as an herb, try finding the flower and wearing or carrying it during the confrontation.

STEPS

1. Place your athame or wand in the dish, and say firmly:

   "Here is the courage.
   Speak the truth.
   Inhale the courage.
   Speak the truth.
   I have the courage
   To speak the truth.
   So mote it be!"

2. Take some of the mixture into your hands and inhale deeply.

3. Before the confrontation, sprinkle some of the mix on your front step or doormat. That way, either you or the person you're confronting will cross it before the conversation happens.

Protection Against a Storm

In these times of global climate change, we're all at risk of facing a catastrophic storm. Here are protective magical steps to take.

SUPPLIES

◆ Hawthorn sticks

NOTES

◆ I've found various woods for magic, including hawthorn, fairly easy to come by online, like on Etsy.

◆ If you're doing this for someone else's home, start at step 4.

STEPS

1. If you performed the "Bless My New Home" spell (page 26), go around to all the doors and windows you blessed and remind them that they have been blessed and purified.

2. If you created the "Anti-Theft Amulet" (page 111), tell it that the storm is a thief that will try to steal into your home.

3. Place a hawthorn stick at/over each door of your home, and one as close as you can get to the roof.

4. Create a protective shield: This is the same as the "Essential All-Purpose Shield" (page 105) but surrounding your home instead of your body.

5. On the top of the shield, visualize a massive umbrella with specific storm-protection powers.

6. Your home is now fully shielded against the storm. Don't forget the bread and milk!

Safe Deployment

This spell is near to my heart. Over the years, my coven heard many pleas: *My brother/cousin/friend is deploying to Afghanistan/Iraq, and I'm so worried.* Using this spell, we kept a half-dozen soldiers in a circle of protection.

SUPPLIES

- Poppet-making materials (page 98)

- An additional smaller dish for consecrated water

NOTES

- Since you're not healing one particular part of the soldier, distribute your protective ingredients throughout the poppet's stuffing.

- Mark the poppet with the warrior's shield rune, Algiz (see illustration), front and back.

- Potential protective ingredients for your poppet include:
  - An iron nail
  - Dill
  - Barley
  - Dried corn
  - Marjoram
  - Aloe

STEPS

1. Create a poppet of the soldier who is deploying.

2. Cast a circle (page 7).

3. After consecrating the elements, put some of the water in the extra dish before mixing salt into the main water dish.

4. After cakes and wine, consecrate the poppet by the four elements, and by the Gods, as in "Method for Distant Healing" (page 96). Ask the Gods you worship for Their aid in protecting this person.

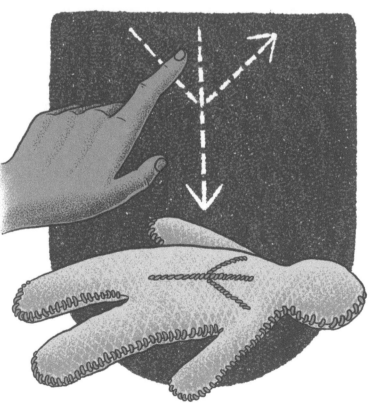

- ◆ Parsley
- ◆ Anise
- ◆ Garlic
- ◆ Woodruff
- ◆ Flint
- ◆ Other herbal protective ingredients similar to dill and marjoram can also be added to the incense. (*Never* burn garlic.) Frankincense, though not specifically protective, can also be used.

5. Place the poppet in front of the altar. Surround it with the four elements: the incense in the East, the censer in the South, the clear water in the extra dish to the West, and the salt to the North.

6. With your strongest tool (sword, athame, staff, or wand), stand over the poppet and draw a circle, East to East, over and over, around the poppet, calling it by the soldier's name:

> *"[Name], I surround you with the circle of protection!*
> *[Name], I surround you with the circle of protection!*
> *[Name], I surround you with the circle of protection!*
> *By Air no harm may come!*
> *From the East no harm may come!*
> *By Fire no harm may come!*
> *From the South no harm may come!*
> *By Water no harm may come!*
> *From the West no harm may come!*
> *By Earth no harm may come!*
> *From the North no harm may come!*
> *From above no harm may come!*
> *From below no harm may come!*
> *So mote it be!"*

7. As you end, draw Algiz over the entire circle of protection the poppet is in.

8. Close the circle (page 8).

How to Remove a Curse

First, know that 90 percent of the time, people who think they're under a curse aren't. The biggest problem I've encountered is cursed *objects*. An object might be purposely cursed, or haunted, or may have picked up negative energy by being near something very bad. Presumably you know this object is cursed because you feel negativity emanate from it. You'll use that sensitivity to determine if your work has been successful.

SUPPLIES

- Pure spring water
- Salt
- Plastic wrap
- A plastic sandwich bag

NOTES

- It's usual to destroy cursed objects. You should still remove the curse before destroying them. Here, we're making an effort to preserve the object.

- Perform steps 1 through 6 during a waning moon.

STEPS

1. Shield yourself thoroughly (page 105).

2. Wash the object in the spring water, visualizing the negativity being washed away.

3. Allow the object to dry in direct, bright sunlight. Sunlight is especially effective for hauntings.

4. If the object can be damaged by salt, wrap it in plastic wrap.

5. Fill the sandwich bag with salt and seal the object into the bag.

6. At night, bury the object. Leave it buried for at least a month.

7. During a waxing moon, return to the burial location. Determine through your psychic sensitivity if the object feels cleansed. If so, unbury it. If not, return again in a month. The worst energies can take a year to remove.

8. After unburying the object, again sense if it is clear. If not, rebury it during a waning moon and repeat the entire process.

Justice in Court

This is for a fair outcome for someone appearing in court. (It's written for you but can be modified for another person.) Don't work this spell if you're in the wrong but want to win anyway.

SUPPLIES

- A representation of the goddess Athena (a statuette or picture of Her or of an owl)
- A dish with an offering to Athena (such as olive oil, bread, olives, meat, fish, or dried grain)
- A dish of spring water
- Olive leaves
- Your athame or wand
- A chopstick or other "invisible writing" implement
- An article of clothing to wear in court

NOTES

- Pure olive oil could be used instead of water and the leaves, but oil can damage clothing.

STEPS

1. Invoke Athena:

   "Athena!
   Beloved gray-eyed Lady of Justice,
   I invoke and call upon you.
   Be here with me, Athena!
   Glorious One,
   Accept my offering,
   And hear my plea.
   See that justice is done!"

2. Hold up the offering and place it before Her.

3. Put the olive leaves into the water.

4. With your athame/wand in the water, say:

   "By the power of Athena
   I invoke justice into this water
   Justice will be done
   So mote it be!"

5. Dip your chopstick in the water and write "JUSTICE" 10 times on the hem, lining, or underside of the garment, repeating *"Justice will be done"* as you do so.

6. After you're done, leave the offering on or near the steps to the courthouse sometime before your case is heard.

7. Dry one of the olive leaves with a towel and carry it with you to court.

Stop the Gossip

Gossip can seem fun and silly when you're engaging in it, but destructive and painful if you're the subject. Here's a spell to silence the gossip.

SUPPLIES

- A "speak no evil" picture or statue
- A censer and charcoal
- Cloves

NOTES

- Everyone has seen the three monkeys: *Hear no evil, speak no evil, see no evil.* Use that image to invoke the silence of "speak no evil."

- Begin the spell during a waning moon on a Monday.

STEPS

1. Place the censer in front of the "speak no evil" picture or statue.

2. Light the charcoal. Place one or two cloves on the censer.

3. Inhale the smoke and say:

   "Power of silence, no evil shall be spoken.
   Power of silence, no evil shall be spoken.
   Power of silence, no evil shall be spoken.
   What I tell you three times is true.
   So mote it be."

4. The next day, find an unburnt piece of clove, or a piece of ash, and take it to the place the gossip is happening. Leave it discreetly there.

5. Repeat this spell every night until the new moon.

CHAPTER 8

Spells of Abundance, Prosperity, and Charity

Prosperity magic can enhance your life. In this chapter, you'll find different ways of bringing in money and abundance, from dealing with and saving money to spells of charity that make acts of giving more plentiful for both the giver and the receiver.

Bringing in Abundance

This section deals with the simple act of making life more abundant: more money, more prosperity, more to share.

Luck and Money Oil

Use this simple potion in any money or prosperity spell. The oil can be used to anoint objects (such as your résumé or a talisman), or add a few drops to a ritual bath or an infuser.

Almond is associated with money, luck, and treasure. Cinnamon is associated with success, money, protection, and love. Both can be found in most grocery stores.

SUPPLIES

♦ A jar with an airtight seal

♦ Whole cinnamon sticks

♦ Enough almond oil to fill your jar

NOTES

♦ Make the potion during a waxing moon.

♦ Cinnamon can irritate sensitive skin and should never be used on small children. Test your own skin before committing to its ritual use.

STEPS

1. Before you begin, breathe deeply, and remind yourself that your purpose is magical.

2. Pack the cinnamon sticks into the jar, whispering *"Success, success, success."*

3. Fill the jar with oil and seal it.

4. Shake the jar thoroughly, again whispering *"Success, success, success."*

5. Place the jar where it can get sunlight, if possible.

6. Shake it every day or two, whispering *"Success, success, success."*

7. The oil will be ready in about four weeks—when the moon returns to the position it was in when you started.

Abundance Cookies: A Sharing Spell

In folklore, food and prosperity are inseparable. Cooking is an act of magic, transforming raw ingredients into something new. And a full stomach is an ancient sign of wealth.

These "Abundance Cookies" will bring abundance to all who eat them—including you. Pecans, almonds, and maple are all associated with wealth. Bring them to a party, a family gathering, or a potluck to "share the wealth."

SUPPLIES

- Maple Cookies (page 130)
- Your athame or wand
- Salt left over from a ritual

NOTES

- Modify your normal ritual preparation to be suitable to the kitchen. For example, if you normally work skyclad, that will not fly.

- The circle around your kitchen is not a full Wiccan circle, which would be impractical. Rather, it consecrates the space for the duration of the cooking.

- Clean your athame or wand thoroughly after the ritual.

STEPS

1. Lay out all your ingredients.

2. Using your athame/wand and your mind's eye, cast a modified circle around the kitchen, declaring:

   "In this space, magic will be made."

3. Holding your athame/wand over the ingredients, say:

   "With these ingredients, magic will be made."

4. Prepare the cookies, being sure the ritual salt is used as an ingredient.

5. When the dough is ready, before baking, plunge your athame/wand in and say:

   "This dough is dough!
   Wealth and fullness!
   So mote it be!"

6. If you like, you can make a dollar sign or other symbol on each cookie before baking.

7. Eat the first cookie as soon as they're ready, in order to trigger the magic.

Maple Cookies

Prep Time: 10 minutes • **Cook Time:** 10 to 12 minutes • **Makes:** 24 cookies

This simple recipe can be used for the Abundance Cookies on page 129.

2½ cups
  all-purpose flour

2 teaspoons
  baking powder

½ teaspoon salt (left
  over from a ritual)

½ cup (1 stick) unsalted
  butter, softened

1 cup light brown sugar

1 large egg,
  room temperature

1½ teaspoons
  vanilla extract

½ cup maple syrup

1. Position a rack in the middle of your oven and preheat the oven to 375°F. Line two baking sheets with parchment paper or silicone baking mats.

2. In a small bowl, whisk together the flour, baking powder, and salt.

3. In a large bowl, using an electric mixer, cream together the butter and sugar until light and fluffy, about 2 minutes.

4. Add the egg and beat well. Add the vanilla and maple syrup and mix until just combined.

5. Gradually beat in the flour mixture.

6. Using a tablespoon, scoop the dough into 1½-inch balls and place them on the baking sheets, leaving about 2 inches between each cookie.

7. Place the baking sheets in the oven on the middle rack and bake for 10 to 12 minutes, or until the cookies are lightly browned on the edges. The centers will look soft. Cool on the baking sheets for 5 minutes. Transfer the cookies to a wire rack to cool completely.

Prosperity Tea

One day while researching herbs, I discovered that both ingredients of my favorite tea are associated with prosperity magic, and so, a spell was born. Tea and bergamot (the ingredients of Earl Grey) are associated with wealth. Honey is associated with prosperity and long life, and bees bring good fortune.

SUPPLIES

- Earl Grey tea

- Honey

NOTES

- Begin this spell on the first Thursday of the waxing moon.

- I recommend getting your tea and honey at a tea specialty shop or a fancier market, if possible, so that the ingredients are fresh and high quality.

STEPS

1. Make a cup of Earl Grey tea, sweetened with honey.

2. As you are about to take your first sip, say:

   "I take abundance into me.
   Abundance comes to me.
   Air, Fire, Water, Earth,
   Abundance comes to me,
   So mote it be."

3. Drink the tea daily, ending at the full moon.

Doorstep Blessing

This spell creates a money-bringing herbal wash to draw money to your front door. These vinegar blends also make a lovely Yule gift for magical friends.

I've offered a variety of ingredients so you can choose scents that appeal to you: Basil and dill create a green, herbal scent. Chamomile and orange are fruity and sweet. Cinnamon and nutmeg have an autumnal aroma.

SUPPLIES

- A bowl

- Ingredients that can include:
    - Fresh basil leaves
    - Chamomile
    - Cinnamon sticks
    - Fresh dill
    - Ground nutmeg
    - Dried orange peel

- Some large bills (twenties at least) and coins

- A saucepan

- White vinegar

- Your wand or athame

- A bottle or jar with a tight seal

- Luck and Money Oil (page 128)

NOTES

- Prepare the mixture on a Thursday just after the new moon, and use it the next Thursday.

STEPS

1. Put your chosen herbal ingredients in the bowl.

2. Mix the herbs and money with your hands, telling the herbs they are coated in money, money is their nature, they are deeply connected with money. *Know* that you are instructing and empowering your ingredients, and they are "catching" wealth from the money in the bowl.

◆ Renew the spell seasonally by rewashing the threshold—reconsecrating the vinegar is not necessary.

3. Fill the jar with the ingredients and coins (keep the bills).

4. Bring the vinegar to a simmer in the saucepan, then carefully pour it into the jar.

5. Point your wand or athame at the jar, sending power as you say:

> *"By the power of the Lady and Lord,*
> *By the power of my will and word,*
> *Money follow where you go,*
> *Money follow where you are,*
> *Money blessings at my door,*
> *So mote it be!"*

6. Let it cool enough to touch, then seal the jar.

7. Use the Luck and Money Oil to mark a pentagram on the jar lid.

8. Store the jar in a dark place for a week.

9. After a week, wipe down your front steps and threshold with the vinegar, concentrating as you do on the abundance it will bring.

Closet Spray

Similar to the "Doorstep Blessing" (page 132), this is a potion to bless your home with prosperity. It is pleasant-smelling and light, so that it can cling to clothing and possessions.

There are enough ingredients listed to let you experiment with the blend for a scent you like. Vetiver and patchouli can be too heavy on their own, but mixed with something light or citrusy, the balance can be delicious. This is a chance to become an amateur perfumer and even add other favorite scents to this mix. Not *all* the ingredients have to be associated with prosperity. In fact, lavender isn't, but, in addition to its love, peace, and relaxation associations, it keeps away clothing moths, so it is ideal for any closet.

SUPPLIES

- Your wand or athame

- Two or more of the following essential oils:

  - Patchouli
  - Vetiver
  - Orange
  - Pineapple
  - Lavender
  - Vervain
  - Orange bergamot

- 91 percent isopropyl (rubbing) alcohol

- Water

- One or more spray bottles

NOTES

- Experimentation with scents should occur before the final spell.

STEPS

1. With your mind clear and focused on magic, gather your ingredients together in the kitchen or bathroom.

2. Visualize riches flowing into your ingredients. These images should be vivid and specific: be sure you understand what prosperity looks like to you before you begin.

3. Direct your wand or athame at the ingredients, sending the images as a stream of power into them, and say:

   "By my will
   Riches flow
   Into this spell
   Riches flow
   By my will
   Money to me
   By my will
   So mote it be!"

- This spell uses essential oils instead of fresh ingredients, for a long-lasting spray that can be reused or given as a gift.

- Create this spray on a Thursday during a waxing moon.

- The rubbing alcohol is a solvent that allows the oils to mix with water, letting the spray diffuse the oils properly. Otherwise, as we all know, oil and water don't mix.

4. Blend a few drops of each selected oil with a 1 part proportion the rubbing alcohol in one of your bottles and shake vigorously.

5. Add 4 parts proportion of water and shake.

6. Spray the mixture lightly into all of your closets, starting at the one nearest your front door and moving deosil through your home.

7. Respray your closets each month on the first Thursday after the new moon.

The Specific Amount Spell

It can be hard for money spells to be effective, in part because they're vague. "I want money" without a clear idea of why, or from where, or how much, is just not how magic works. By contrast, this spell is often incredibly effective. Do this spell when an exact dollar amount is needed for a specific purpose, such as a rent shortfall of $212 or an electric bill of $86.

SUPPLIES

♦ A blank check

♦ Your magic pen

♦ Luck and Money Oil (page 128)

NOTES

♦ If you don't have a check, use a printout of the payment page of whatever e-source you use to pay bills.

♦ Perform this spell during a waxing moon.

STEPS

1. Wetting your finger with the Luck and Money Oil, anoint the edges of the check, leaving the writing area clear. Know that you have created a magical object of this check.

2. With your magic pen, fill in the amount needed and the person owed. Date the check with the due date for the debt.

3. Again wetting your finger with Luck and Money Oil, trace over the amount. Repeat this nine times, while saying:

   *"Three times three
   Money comes to me."*

4. End with *"So mote it be!"*

5. Leave the check where you can see it. Every time you see it, say the amount, and repeat

   *"Three times three
   Money comes to me."*

The Paystub Spell

This spell blesses your paystub. Since the paystub is a physical representation of the money you already earn, and will earn in the future, it can be a powerful magical talisman. This spell can be performed outdoors in a garden, or indoors with a potted plant.

SUPPLIES

- Your paystub
- Luck and Money Oil (page 128)
- A plant/seedling
- Plant pot or garden soil
- Tools for planting (trowel, watering can, gardening gloves)

NOTES

- If you don't receive a physical paystub, you can print one from your payroll company's website.
- Perform this spell in the late spring or early summer (planting season) in a waxing moon.

STEPS

1. Anoint the paystub with Luck and Money Oil, and say:

   "The fruit of my work
   The seed I plant
   Grow seed grow
   Your fruit is sweet."

2. Dig deep into the pot or garden soil, and "plant" the paystub, repeating the spell as you do.

3. Put some soil on top of the paystub, and then plant the seedling on top of it, again repeating the spell.

4. Nurture and care for this plant throughout the growing season.

Dealing with Money

Sometimes the problem isn't *bringing* money, but *handling* it. Some of us have no education about money, and saving, investing, and basic understanding can be a challenge. Some people have emotional baggage regarding money, possessions, and prosperity, and that can prevent us from doing as well as we should financially.

Spell for Saving

Some people are hoarders, while others cannot hold on to anything. This spell helps you hoard in a healthy way, to build a savings account. Before you begin, go to a physical or online bank and open a savings account. Also, write up a plan as to how you will save—how frequently you will contribute how much, and how you will make that happen. Remember that magic works *with* real-world action, not *instead* of it.

SUPPLIES

- Some stones, from your garden or found in nature—any that appeal to you and feel earthy

- A green, brown, black, or red cord

- A statement or printout from your savings account

NOTES

- Perform this spell on a Saturday during the waxing moon.

STEPS

1. Cast a circle (page 7).

2. When you consecrate the elements, include the stones in the Earth consecration, placing them temporarily in the salt dish.

3. After cakes and wine, ask the Gods you worship to help you develop a meaningful savings account that you contribute to regularly.

4. Consecrate the cords by the four elements, and say:

   "Air and Fire / Water and Earth, consecrate this tool of magic that binds me to the commitment I make."

◆ For the cord, choose the color you think best represents this magic: green is money; green, black, and brown can all represent Earth; and red is the life force.

5. Now consecrate the bank statement by the four elements, and say:

    "Air and Fire/Water and Earth, consecrate this tool of finance that holds and keeps the commitment I make."

6. Stand and pick up the stones. Rub yourself all over, head to toe, feeling yourself grounded and connected to Earth as you do so. Visualize buried treasure, and gold mines, and all the ways that Earth helps you hold, save, and store treasure.

7. Hold the statement in your non-dominant hand (e.g., the left if you're right-handed). Use the cord to bind the statement to you, repeating as you do:

    "I am bound to save."

8. End with *"So mote it be."*

9. Close the circle (page 8).

Get a Job!

This spell is designed to bring you an ideal job, as defined by you. The kind you'll stick with, that will reward you financially and personally.

SUPPLIES

- Luck and Money Oil (page 128)

- A green candle, dressed (page 13)

- A printed copy of your résumé

- An envelope

- Your magical writing pen

NOTES

- Perform this spell during a waxing moon.

- An ideal rhyme is one suited to your ideal job. Change the words as needed.

- Come up with a sigil for the new job, such as a bind rune (page 36) or a glyph that represents the work you do (like a badge for police work). Have this in mind before you begin.

STEPS

1. Cast the circle (page 7). Invoke a God or Goddess with a connection to your career path, such as Hermes for communication, or Bast for nursing.

2. After cakes and wine, assemble all your supplies on the altar. Light the candle.

3. Ask the Gods you've invoked to bless the work you are about to do.

4. Visualize your ideal job. Hold the image clearly in your mind.

5. With that image firmly in your mind, cense the résumé and say:

   "By Air and Fire, the job is mine."
   Then wet it with saltwater, and say:
   "By Water and Earth, the job is mine."

6. Dip your finger in the Luck and Money Oil and draw your sigil on the résumé, repeating your rhyme over and over:

   "The sun does shine
   The job is mine
   The moon does glow
   To work I go."

7. Gaze at the candle. Allow yourself to be drawn into the flame. Breathing deeply, again bring the image of the job and see it in the flame. Recite your rhyme over and over, gradually letting the tempo and the intensity increase, holding the image at all times. At peak, send all your power into the résumé, visualizing the energy pushing it, and you, directly into the ideal job.

8. Fold your résumé and put it in the envelope. Seal the envelope and address it to *"Terrific Employer, Excellent Location"* (or something like that—don't send it to a real address and don't include a return address).

9. Close the circle (page 8).

10. Put the envelope in a mailbox as soon as possible.

Release the Block

Sometimes we get stuck. Maybe our job is a dead end, or we don't know how to stick to a budget. We might not know what's stopping us, but it seems something is. This spell is designed to release a blockage. Most money-oriented spells use Earth, for wealth, stability, and security. But here you need Water, for cleansing as well as "going with the flow." Sesame is associated with money, and with unlocking doors—a good symbol for this spell.

SUPPLIES

♦ Sesame seeds in a dish

♦ Your wand or athame

♦ A pitcher of water

NOTES

♦ Perform this spell in a waning moon.

STEPS

1. Point your athame/wand into the seeds and begin naming your blocks. You might say, "I don't know how to change my career," or "I just can't seem to get ahead and I don't know why." Speak freely and say as much as you need to say. Fill the seeds with your blocks.

2. Point your athame/wand into the water pitcher and say:

   "Water cleanse me,
   Water clear the way!
   As the waves turn rock to sand,
   Water, clear the way!
   As the flood breaks down the dam,
   Water, clear the way!
   As the rain washes clear the land,
   Water, clear the way!"

3. Take the seeds and water into the shower. Pour the seeds over yourself, noticing how they stick to your skin. Some fall away at once, but some cling.

4. Turn on the shower. Mix the consecrated pitcher water with the shower water, washing away these blocks. Allow yourself to feel truly cleansed. The flowing water is clearing the way.

5. Watch the tiny seeds going down the drain, knowing your blocks, too, are going down the drain.

Charity Spells

These spells emphasize giving, although the truth is, the division between giving and receiving is artificial. Generosity creates abundance, as we participate in the ebb and flow of a universe that gives to us all.

Magic Coins

This spell blesses a batch of coins that can then be given away—whenever you see a charity box or a tip jar, drop a coin in and let the magic grow.

SUPPLIES

◆ An assortment of coins in a dish

NOTES

◆ If you want to use your wand or athame to consecrate the coins, hold the tool in your hand as you raise power.

STEPS

1. Cast the circle (page 7).

2. After cakes and wine, ask the Gods you worship to bless your work with abundance.

3. Consecrate the dish of coins by the four elements, and say:

   "Air and Fire/Water and Earth, make this money grow wherever it shall go!"

4. Raise power by drumming, dancing, chanting, spinning, or whatever appeals to you. All the while, chant:

   *"Give and receive, ebb and flow
   Money grows wherever it goes!"*

5. At peak, plunge your athame/wand/hands into the dish of coins, shouting:

   "So mote it be!"

6. Close the circle (page 8).

CONTINUED ▶

Magic Coins (continued)

7. Immediately after the circle, throw one coin far away (even out your window) so that the magic begins to spread at once.

8. Carry the coins with you, dropping them in charity boxes, collections, and tip jars, wherever you go. Each time, you can whisper, *"Money grows wherever it goes."*

Giveaway Blessings

From time to time, I give clothing to Goodwill or another charity. If this is something you also do, adding a blessing to that donation is a way to increase the good you do.

SUPPLIES

- The clothing to be donated
- Your wand or athame
- Cedar incense
- Saltwater
- Closet Spray (page 134) (optional)
- Magic Coins (page 143) (optional)

NOTES

- Perform this spell during a waxing moon.
- You are not doing this spell *in* a cast circle, because the circle is around the clothing, not you.

STEPS

1. Place the clothing in the center of your normal circle space.

2. Meditate on the ways a donation can help: Think about protecting those in need, about housing and shelter and stability.

3. Draw a circle around the clothing with your wand or athame, from East to East, and say:

   "I surround this gift with protective power.
   Where this gift goes, charity flowers.
   Protection, home, stability,
   As I do say, so mote it be."

4. Cense around the circle, and say:

   "Air, bring clarity and vision to this gift
   And those who receive it
   Fire, bring passion and power to this gift
   And those who receive it."

5. Sprinkle saltwater around the circle, and say:

   "Water, bring compassion and kindness to this gift
   And those who receive it
   Earth, bring safety and protection to this gift
   And those who receive it.
   So mote it be."

6. If using, the clothing lightly with the closet spray, and/or put magic coins in pockets of various garments.

7. Package and donate the clothing as soon as possible after doing this spell.

Celebrating the Seasons
and the Land

Wicca is known as a nature religion, and connection to nature's cycles is an essential part of this path. If you live in the city or suburbs, it's easy to be disconnected from nature, and even easier to romanticize it. But Nature in Her true form—hard and demanding, as well as beautiful—is available to all of us. We are all connected to the seasons and can deepen that connection through ritual.

This chapter contains a basic round of Wiccan lunar and solar celebrations—Esbats and Sabbats—as well as other rites related to the land.

Sabbats and Esbats

These ceremonies sit at the very core of Wicca; we mark the times of the moon and the seasons of the Sun. If we do nothing else, no spells, no charms, no prayers or potions, these rites alone can keep us deeply in tune with what it means to be Wiccan.

If you can't do a ritual on the exact day of the moon or holiday, it's better to do it before, when the energy is rising, rather than after, when the energy is falling. To create any seasonal or lunar rite, use the basic circle casting and closing (page 7–8), and adjust it to the occasion.

The Full Moon

To me, to commune with the full moon is the heart and soul of being Wiccan. What I offer here is an outline that I hope you will expand upon through the experience of passionate worship, Moon after Moon.

The scientifically proven effects of the full moon last three days, from the day before to the day after. A rite performed on any of those days is legitimately a "full moon rite."

SUPPLIES

◆ None, other than what you use to cast a circle

NOTES

◆ Ideally, this ritual is performed outdoors, by moonlight. If working indoors, I go out and gaze at the moon before coming in for my rite.

◆ At lunar rites, moon cakes (plain white cakes shaped like the moon) are appropriate.

STEPS

1. Cast the circle (page 7). At "Declare Intention," say:

   "We are/I am here tonight to worship and honor the Lady of the Moon in Her fullness."

2. When you call the quarters, add "of the full moon":

   "I call Air/Fire/Water/Earth to guard this sacred circle of the full moon in the East/South/West/North! Blessed be!"

3. When you invoke the Goddess and God, be specific about the full moon. Here is where you can be poetic, heartfelt, and as elaborate as you like. Describe the moon, Her beauty, how it feels to gaze at Her, and how the God Himself adores Her beauty.

   ◆ Imagery associated with the full moon that can be part of your invocation includes: beauty, fullness, brightness, motherhood, daughterhood, pregnancy, silver, menstruation, secret lovers, priestesses, and diadems.

   ◆ Goddesses associated with the full moon include Selene, Diana, Aradia, Isis, Arianrhod, and Melusine.

   ◆ Moon Gods include Shiva, Khonsu, and Thoth (it is not necessary to invoke both a Goddess and a God of the moon—many Gods worship and adore the Moon Goddess).

4. At the offering, and through cakes and wine, again specify that you are worshipping the Full Moon and this is a gift to Her.

5. Magic done at this time should be about worship, fullness, and completion. Or just worship and save magic for waning and waxing moons.

6. Closing the circle (page 8) needs no special modification.

The New Moon

The New Moon is a time of darkness and mystery. Some Wiccans don't do New Moon circles. I find it's convenient to have another day to worship "once in the month," and so I've learned to explore the mysteries of the darkness. It's also the first day before the fortuitous waxing moon begins, and so is a time of power. Because the moon isn't visible at this time, nothing in your rite should emphasize beauty. Rather, speak of the inner qualities and innate powers of the Goddess.

SUPPLIES

◆ None, other than what you use to cast a circle

NOTES

◆ At lunar rites, moon cakes (plain white cakes shaped like the moon) are appropriate.

STEPS

1. Cast the circle (page 7). At "Declare Intention," say:

   "At the dark of the moon, I/we draw inward, seeking wisdom from the darkness, seeking wisdom from the Lady of the Dark and Her beloved Consort."

2. When you call the quarters, say:

   "I call Air/Fire/Water/Earth to guard this sacred circle of the new moon in the East/South/West/North! Blessed be!"

3. When you invoke the Goddess and God, be specific about the new moon. Now is the time to invoke secrets and mysteries. Now is the time to reveal the hidden, and to speak to the Lady from Whom nothing is hidden. Invoke Her wisdom and knowledge.

   ◆ Imagery associated with the new moon that can be part of your invocation includes: Darkness, secrets, mystery, crossroads, wisdom, banishing, and witchcraft.

   ◆ Goddesses associated with the new moon include Hecate, Isis, Cerridwen, Nuit, and Nyx.

4. At the offering, and through cakes and wine, again specify that you are worshipping the New Moon and this is a gift to Her.

5. Magic done at this time should be about uncovering secrets—this is an excellent time for divination. Witchcraft itself is associated with the new moon.

6. Closing the circle (page 8) needs no special modification.

Creating the Seasonal Circle

Like life passages (page 18), seasonal rites follow a template. The eight sabbats of the Wiccan "Wheel of the Year" all use this pattern. This also allows you to quickly and easily modify rites to suit your taste.

The Wheel of the Year is:

Beltane: May 1
Midsummer: Summer Solstice (about June 21)
Lughnasadh (also known as Lammas): August 1
Harvest Home: Fall Equinox (about September 21)
Samhain: October 31
Yule: Winter Solstice (about December 21)
Imbolc (also known as Oilmelc, Brigid, Candlemas): February 1
Ostara (also known as Lady Day): Spring Equinox (about March 21)

Many of these festivals relate to fertility. Modern Pagans understand that fertility doesn't necessarily mean having babies. Writing is fertile, while writer's block is barren. The things we create are things we "give birth to." Of course, "fertile" also means enough to eat, and the need for sustenance hasn't changed with modernity.

SUPPLIES

♦ Vary by the specific rite. At minimum, decorate the altar in a seasonal manner.

♦ Some people create seasonal altar clothes, candleholder, robes, and even special seasonal tools!

STEPS

1. Cast the circle (page 7). At "Declare Intention," name or describe the sabbat. A longer description, song, or poetry about the sabbat can be part of the opening declaration.

2. At "Call the Quarters," add the sabbat to your invocation:

    "I call Air/Fire/Water/Earth to guard this [sabbat] circle in the East/South/West/North! Blessed be!"

3. At "Invoke the Gods," you can invoke specific deities associated with the holiday—some people use a different pair for each sabbat. Or, you can invoke the same deities you always worship, but with an emphasis on who They are at this time of year. For example, the Stag God has antlers that shed each spring and regrow, so describing His antlers is meaningful. The Gods and Goddesses of Wicca are seasonal beings, different in the winter and summer, and are invoked differently.

4. At "Give an Offering," the entire offering should be seasonal. In fact, it is in this section where most of the difference per occasion is found.

   Often, a sabbat rite is theatrical, with a performance representing the season—candles snuffed in the darkness of Samhain, birth enacted at Yule, the Goddess awakening in the spring. These performances are the offering given to the Gods and Goddesses.
   Some people do a different enactment/celebration each year; the creation of a new ceremony is part of how they celebrate and how they honor the Gods and Goddesses. Others do the same rite each year, sometimes with variation.

5. Sometimes the enactment/celebration continues into cakes and wine.

6. Traditionally, no magic is done at the sabbats. Instead, use the time after cakes and wine for seasonal games, story-telling, songs, or (especially at Samhain) divination.

7. The only needed variation in closing the circle is to thank the same Gods and Goddesses you invoked. You can again mention the occasion.

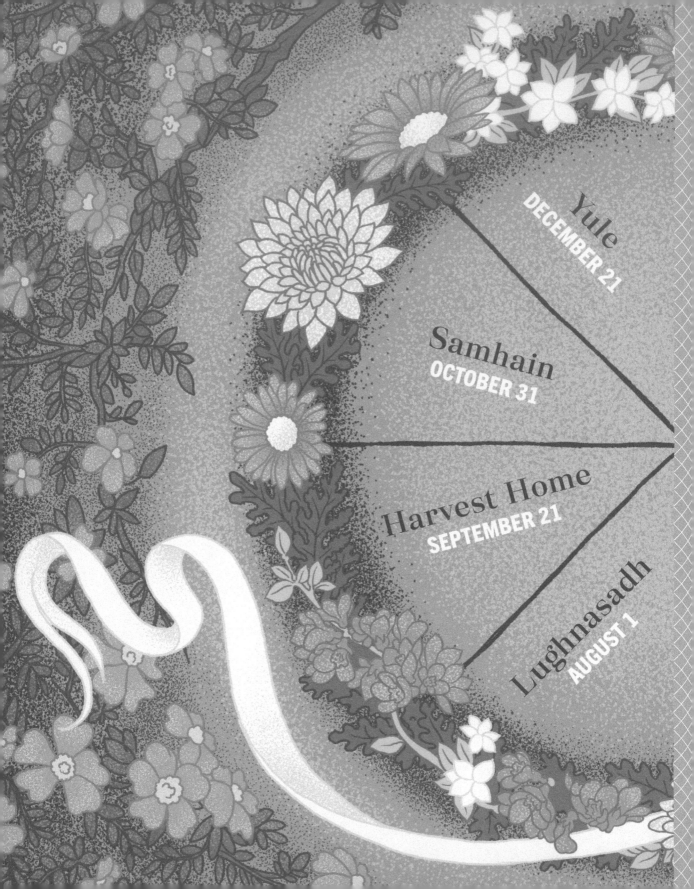

Yule
DECEMBER 21

Samhain
OCTOBER 31

Harvest Home
SEPTEMBER 21

Lughnasadh
AUGUST 1

Imbolc
FEBRUARY 1

Ostara
MARCH 21

Beltane
MAY 1

Midsummer
JUNE 21

Beltane (May Day)

Beltane is traditionally when outdoor fun (of both the family-friendly and adult-only varieties) begins. It is a celebration of play and sexuality, and of the rebirth and renewal of the fertile earth. It unites God and Goddess, bringing fulfillment to all. In ancient Ireland, cattle were driven between fires to purify them, and couples leapt over fires to promote fertility.

SUPPLIES

- Material for building and safely extinguishing a fire

- A wreath or circlet to use as a headdress

- Multicolored ribbons

- Abundant fresh flowers and ribbons for decoration, (optional) erotic symbols on the altar

- A rattle or other handheld instrument

NOTES

- Have a small fire going before you begin. If you can't build a fire outside, place candles in a cauldron (or a fireproof substitute) to simulate the balefire.

STEPS

1. At "Declare Intention," say:

   "Welcome the May! Welcome fruitfulness!
   Welcome, O glorious love between Lady and Lord.
   Shine Your abundance on me as I worship You on this sacred day.
   Welcome and blessed be."

   Meditate on the coming season. Feel the spring moving in, warming you. Put on your headdress.

2. At "Invoke the Gods," raise your wand into the air and invoke:

   "Glorious Lady of Flowers
   Fill the land with Your joy
   Beloved Lady of Abundance
   Join me to celebrate Your renewal."

   Walk to the fire you have built, raise your wand over it, and say:
   "Mighty Stag Lord
   Come and join Your Lady
   Beloved Horned One
   Dance the sacred dance with us
   Purify the fire that all may be renewed."

- If you're celebrating with a group, create and dance around a maypole instead of using the ribbon headdress. The maypole dance is usually done before the circle is cast. The wrapped pole then stands at the center of the circle.

- Use the Seasonal Circle template for each step (page 154).

3. At "Give an Offering," place your beribboned headdress on the altar. Meditate on how the ribbons represent the Lady and Lord. Begin braiding your ribbons, knowing you are weaving Their union into your headdress, bringing their joined energies into yourself.

Put your headdress back on. Choose a song to sing, and begin dancing around the circle with your rattle. When you are ready, get a running start and jump over the fire! Continue dancing and leaping until you are exhausted.

4. For cakes and wine, consecrate cakes and wine directly over the fire, pouring your offering into the flames.

5. Close the circle (page 8).

6. After closing, be sure the fire is safely and thoroughly doused.

Midsummer

Summer Solstice is the longest day of the year, and celebrates the Sun God at His peak. It's also a seashore festival. If you live anywhere near the shore, that's an ideal place to celebrate.

Decorate with sun symbols and representations of the Goddess, like seashells or flowers.

SUPPLIES

- Material for building and safely extinguishing a fire
- Your braided headdress from Beltane (page 158)
- Two simple masks (one gold, one black)
- A rattle or other handheld instrument

NOTES

- Prepare an outdoor or indoor fire, as at Beltane.
- If working indoors, set aside the headdress as a sacrifice and burn it outdoors at a later time.
- Remove anything that can't be burned from the headdress in advance of the rite.
- The rite can easily be adapted for a group.
- Use the Seasonal Circle template for each step (page 154).

STEPS

1. At "Declare Intention," say:

   "I celebrate the longest day of the year. The Sun Lord is at His peak, and the Dark Lord nips at His heels." Meditate on the days growing shorter. As summer seems just to begin, the seeds of its end are already planted.

2. At "Invoke the Gods," raise your wand into the air and invoke:

   "Lord of the Sun, brightness of days
   Come on the longest day to be adored
   Lord of the Sun, before You begin to wane
   Come and dance with me!
   Lord who is Two, join me!

   Lady of the Sea, Lady of the Flowers
   The Sun dies and is reborn, but You are eternal
   Your lover dies, Your lover is born, Your love is eternal.

   Welcome and blessed be."

3. At "Give an Offering," put on the solar mask and feel the energy of the Sun God enter you. Say:

   "I am the Sun and the Stag. Today is My day. Today is the longest day. My energies brighten the world."

   Dance once around the circle. When you return to the altar, pick up the headdress. Dance with it to the fire, and throw it in.

Remove your gold mask and put on your black mask. Walk slowly once around the circle. Say:

> "I am the Night and the Bull. Tonight is My night.
> Tomorrow the day is shorter, and I begin to grow.
> I whisper secrets to the world."

4. At cakes and wine, take the cup and athame/wand to the fire, consecrate cakes and wine, and say:

   > "The Stag and Bull worship and adore the Eternal Mother, and pour Our offerings out to Her."
   > Pour an offering into the flames.

5. Close the circle (page 8).

6. After closing, be sure the fire is safely and thoroughly doused.

Lughnasadh

Lughnasadh is the first of three agricultural harvests. It is a grain harvest, and venerates John Barleycorn—the God in the Grain, who dies (is harvested) and is reborn (as bread) that we may live. Decorate with wheat, corn, and local produce.

Note: Folklore associates John Barleycorn with beer (of which barley is an ingredient) as well as grain. If this is uncomfortable for you, naturally you can choose a different God for this rite.

One beautiful tradition is to bake your own bread at Lughnasadh. The experience of pounding down dough and then seeing it rise connects you to the cycle of grain-to-bread-to-us that is venerated at this time.

Lughnasadh is also a time for large gatherings of Pagans for games and competitions, and attending a local Pagan Pride is reminiscent of this tradition.

SUPPLIES

+ A loaf of bread (preferably freshly baked) on a tray (see page 164 for recipe)

+ A cloth to cover the bread

NOTES

+ Beer, since it's made from grain, is preferable to wine.

+ Use the Seasonal Circle template for each step (page 154).

STEPS

1. At "Declare Intention," say:

   "This is Lughnasadh, the day of the Grain God."

2. At "Invoke the Gods," raise your wand into the air and invoke:

   "John Barleycorn, I worship You
   You who rise and fall, rise and fall
   Be here to teach me the wisdom of change
   Be here in Your rebirth!

   Gracious Mother, fertile Earth
   You hold the wheat as it grows
   You hold the wheat as it is cut down
   Bless us with Your bounty!

   Welcome and blessed be."

3. At "Give an Offering," hold the covered tray before you. Meditate on the meaning of bread. It is the root of civilization, it is sacrifice, and it is rebirth.

Say:

> *"This is the funeral of John Barleycorn. The God has been cut down."*

Carry the tray three times around the circle. Return to the altar. Remove the cloth and say:

> *"John Barleycorn is reborn!"*

4. For cakes and wine, hold the cup directly over the loaf when performing cakes and wine (or "cakes and ale") and allow a bit of drink to spill on the bread.

5. Close the circle (page 8).

White Sandwich Bread

Prep Time: 20 minutes, plus 1 hour 30 minutes to rise
Cook Time: 30 minutes • **Makes:** 2 (9-by-5-inch) loaves

Fresh-baked bread is a meaningful way to honor John Barleycorn at Lughnasadh, and this simple recipe is accessible even for a first-time baker. You can gift the second loaf to another harvest celebrant.

¼ cup granulated sugar

2 cups warm water (105 to 110°F)

1½ tablespoons active dry yeast

¼ cup vegetable oil

6 cups bread flour

1½ teaspoons salt

1. In a large bowl, using a wooden spoon (or in the bowl of your stand mixer with the dough hook attachment), dissolve the sugar in the warm water. Stir in the yeast. Let stand until the yeast resembles a creamy foam, about 10 minutes.

2. Add the oil, flour, and salt. Mix until the flour has been incorporated and the dough comes away from the bowl. Place the dough on a lightly floured surface and knead for about 10 minutes (or on low in a stand mixer for 5 minutes). Place the dough in a lightly greased bowl and turn once to coat. Cover the bowl with a clean dish towel or plastic wrap and let rise until doubled in size, about 1 hour.

3. Punch down the dough and divide it in half. Roll out each half into a rectangle. Starting on the long side, roll up each half, tucking the ends underneath the loaves. Place each loaf into a greased 9-by-5-inch loaf pan. Allow to rise for 30 minutes, or until dough has risen 1 inch above pans.

4. Near the end of the rising time, preheat the oven to 350°F and position a rack in the middle of the oven.

5. Bake the loaves on the middle rack for 30 minutes, or until golden brown on top and an instant-read thermometer reads 190°F. Cool completely on a wire rack before slicing.

Harvest Home

This second harvest festival is a bit like a Wiccan Thanksgiving. It's both a wonderful time for a feast and a time of reflection. As temperatures cool, we draw inward. We see summer ending and plan for what's next. Since feasting is appropriate, you might prepare a big meal in advance to enjoy in the circle. Use autumnal decorations like leaves and gourds.

SUPPLIES

- None, other than what you use to cast a circle

NOTES

- Incense is a traditional offering. It requires a charcoal and loose incense, not sticks.

- Choose a harvest chant, such as "Hoof and Horn."

- Use the Seasonal Circle template for each step (page 154).

STEPS

1. At "Declare Intention," say:

   "At Harvest Home, day and night are equal. Now we mark the shift from warmth to coolness, and give thanks."

2. At "Invoke the Gods," raise your wand into the air and invoke:

   "Lady and Lord, thank You for the abundant harvest!
   You have given me food when I might hunger,
   You have given me shelter when I might be homeless,
   I am grateful to You, beloved Lady, beloved Lord, for all You provide,
   Be here to celebrate the Harvest with me.
   Welcome and blessed be."

3. At "Give an Offering," chant and dance around the circle. As you go from East (Spring) to South (Summer) to West (Autumn) to North (Winter), see your dance as the progression of the seasons.

   Stand between South and West: the progression of Summer to Autumn. Meditate on all you are thankful for, on all the abundance that Nature has provided. Take a pinch of incense and drop it on the censer, and say:

   "I give thanks for the blessing of [name a blessing in your life]."

CONTINUED ▶

Harvest Home (continued)

Repeat this for as many blessings in your life as you feel appropriate, taking in the growing smoke that represents your blessings. Then add a final pinch and say:

"I give thanks for the blessings yet to come."

4. While cakes and wine is normally a simple drink and a bit of bread or cake, tonight a full feast is appropriate. Enjoy!

5. Close the circle (page 8).

Samhain

Samhain (pronounced SOW-wen) is the Feast of the Dead, as well as the last harvest. It is the time of culling the herd and preparing against the frost. Traditional foods are pork, apples, and squashes, all harvested or slaughtered at this time. Decorate with pumpkins, apples, and Halloween-themed items.

This is the time to honor your beloved dead. They can be human or animal, family or friends. They can be people who influenced you but whom you did not know: spiritual ancestors. (Many modern Wiccans honor Gerald Gardner as an ancestor.) Don't feel obligated to honor dead relatives who were abusive or hurtful.

SUPPLIES

- Pictures and mementos of your beloved dead
- A table, stand, or tray on which to display them
- An extra pair of white candles
- A second incense holder
- An apple, and a knife to cut it
- A second cup
- A feast of traditional foods

NOTES

- Prepare an ancestor altar in the West, with the extra candles and incense, the cup, and all the mementos.

STEPS

1. At "Declare Intention," say:

   "Tonight, when the veil between the worlds of the living and the dead is most thin, I celebrate the Feast of the Ancestors, and welcome my honored dead."

2. At "Invoke the Gods," raise your wand into the air and invoke:

   "Mighty Horned One, You who wear the crown of the Underworld, I do not fear You. I know You bring peace and rest from the journey. Join my circle.
   Beloved Lady, on this night You pass from the fertile Earth to join Your beloved Lord in the world below. I know You will return, for You leave Your promise in the apple. Join my circle.
   Lord and Lady, be here, this Samhain night, to celebrate the honored dead with me.
   Welcome and blessed be."

CONTINUED ▶

Samhain (continued)

- Place the apple before your image of the Goddess.

- Use the Seasonal Circle template for each step (page 154).

3. At "Give an Offering," light the candles and incense on the ancestor altar. Say:

   "In this magic circle, a place not a place, a time out of time, I can commune with my beloved dead."

   Name each person represented on your altar. Speak freely to them. Think about and express why you choose to honor them. It's okay to cry, and it's also okay to be happy—this is a reunion.

4. For cakes and wine, consecrate the wine with the athame as usual. Slice the apple in half horizontally, revealing the Goddess hidden within. Say:

   "Lady, I know you are with me, because I see you here. Blessed be."

   Consecrate the remaining food.

   Bring half the apple and the wine to the ancestor altar. Say:

   "Eat and drink with me. Let's celebrate together."

   Pour a toast to each ancestor, adding anyone you want, whether on the altar or not. Eat your feast with your ancestors. Be sure to place their portion outside on the earth after the ritual is over.

5. Close the circle (page 8).

Yule

This is a joyous time, the rebirth of the Sun God. It is the longest night; days begin to grow hereafter. At Summer Solstice we celebrate the two-faced God as two powerful men. At Winter Solstice, we see Him as an infant and an old man. Celebrations of birth and motherhood are common. Some Pagans keep vigil throughout the longest night, to watch for the rebirth of the Sun. Decorate with traditional Yuletide decor, especially stars, lights, and solar symbols. The Old God/dying year can be represented by a bearded old Santa, if you like.

SUPPLIES

◆ An extra white candle (one per person if a group), by the altar

◆ A hand-drum or rattle

◆ A cauldron (or fireproof substitute) with about 2 inches of sand

NOTES

◆ Start with your quarter candles unlit—the circle should be dark to represent the longest night.

◆ Any extra candles used as decor should be lit when the quarter candles are lit.

◆ You can use a large, pillar-style candle for the cauldron and let it burn overnight, provided you use plenty of sand for fire safety.

STEPS

1. At "Declare Intention," say:

   "On the longest night, I celebrate the rebirth of the Sun. In darkness, I have faith He will come to light my way."

2. At "Invoke the Gods," raise your wand into the air and invoke:

   "Beloved Mother, be here with Your love to light the darkest night. Be here, giving birth to the holy Sun, that I may adore Him.
   Bright Lord, be born, here, to Your adoring worshipper. Return with light for all.
   Welcome and blessed be."

3. At "Give an Offering," meditate in the darkness. Briefly contemplate all the things in your life that seem darkest and most hopeless. Let the feeling of darkness wash over you, and say:

   "Lady and Lord! I cannot live in darkness! I know light must return! I know I am not abandoned! I know if I last through the longest night, the dawn will come. In darkness, there is light. In despair, there is hope. In the darkest soil of winter, there is the seed of spring. So mote it be!"

CONTINUED ▶

Yule (continued)

◆ Use the Seasonal Circle
template for each step
(page 154).

Light the white candle, and say:

"The light is reborn! Blessed be the Sun!"

Light the quarter candles, starting from the East, and
any other candles, repeating *"The light is reborn! Blessed
be the Sun!"* with each lit candle.

Place the white candle in the cauldron. Get your rattle
and dance around the cauldron of flame,
celebrating the rebirth of the Sun.

4. Close the circle (page 8).

Imbolc

In the depth of winter, Imbolc celebrates spring. It is when ewes begin to lactate; milk is often a part of this festival. It is also the feast day of the Goddess Brigid, Lady of Inspiration. She rules the three fires: Healing (fire of the body), smithcraft (fire of the forge), and inspiration (fire of the head). Decorate with green for Brigid, red for fire, white for milk; use cows, cauldrons, and metals as themes. This ritual is written for Brigid, but other seasonal rites incorporate Groundhog Day (which looks to the coming spring), or Valentine's Day (which awakens love in a time of darkness).

SUPPLIES

◆ Three green or red candles

◆ A cauldron (or fireproof substitute)

◆ Materials for whatever creative art you choose, such as a pen and paper for writing, or needles and yarn for knitting

NOTES

◆ Use milk or Irish cream instead of wine.

◆ The invocation mentions "poetry and song." Substitute whatever arts or crafts are meaningful to you.

◆ Use the Seasonal Circle template for each step (page 154).

STEPS

1. At "Declare Intention," say:

   "I celebrate Imbolc, Brigid's Day, and honor the sacred fires."

2. At "Invoke the Gods," raise your wand into the air and invoke:

   "Brigid, be welcome here. Come to my circle. Lady of inspiration, fill my head with poetry and song. I celebrate You in the lamb and calves, in the fire, and in my heart.
   Mighty Horned One, You who are in the sleeping seed, You who fill the bellies of the ewes and cows, come to my circle.
   Welcome and blessed be."

3. At "Give an Offering," light the three candles in the cauldron. Say:

   "Brigid, Lady of Fire, fill my cauldron, fill my mind, fill my body."

   Meditate on the area of your life that needs inspiration, and feel the fire entering and inspiring you.

   Say: *"Brigid, I offer my creativity to You."*

   Use the creative tools you've brought into the circle.

4. Close the circle (page 8).

Ostara

Spring Equinox stands opposite Harvest Home. Again, day and night are equal. Now it's time to plant the seeds anticipated in the fall (the "blessings yet to come"). The Germanic goddess Ostara (or Eostre) is associated with the Spring Equinox and coming warmth. Her name is the origin of the word "Easter." Decorate with colored eggs and ribbons.

SUPPLIES

- A white candle
- A bowl with seeds that can be planted at this time of year (mustard, peas, and daisies in temperate zones)
- A bowl of soil
- Colored eggs for "cakes" (optional)

NOTES

- Use the Seasonal Circle template for each step (page 154).

STEPS

1. At "Declare Intention," say:

   "I welcome Spring on this day. The Goddess warms the Earth. The God fertilizes the seeds. Life returns!"

2. At "Invoke the Gods," raise your wand into the air and invoke:

   "Maiden of Earth, Lady of new life, be here in my circle!
   Fair one, bringer of joy and renewal, break the winter's silence!
   Laughing God of the greenwood, be here in my circle!
   Shepherd of creatures wild and free, dance here with Your cloven hooves.
   Let life be born anew!
   Welcome and blessed be."

3. At "Give an Offering," light the candle, and say:

   "Life is reborn. Day will be longer than night. Darkness is defeated."

   Lift your athame over the seeds, flowing your energy through the blade into the seeds, and say:
   "Thus does the God fertilize the Earth."
   Plunge your athame into the seeds.
   Lift the dish of seeds high, and say: *"And the Goddess does accept His blessings."*

Take one seed and plant it in the bowl of soil with a wish for something you want to grow or be born in the coming season. Repeat this, with a new wish, for each seed you plant.

4. During cakes and wine, you can eat colored eggs with (or instead of) your cakes.

5. After you close the circle and the ritual is complete, plant the seeds outdoors, if you can.

Land Rites

Wicca can deepen our sense of connection to the land, simply by practicing rites that mark the seasons. We know the tides of moon and sun and come to attune ourselves to them. We can also improve our relationship to the land with simple rites and spells, like the ones that follow.

Bless This Garden

To promote health and growth in your garden, use this spell when you first turn the soil. The mixture can be reused throughout the growing season. Apples and cider have a long history of use blessing gardens.

SUPPLIES

- Apple cider in a large goblet or bowl

- A bottle or jar

NOTES

- Perform this spell during a waxing moon.

- Keep the mixture refrigerated between uses.

STEPS

1. Cast the circle (page 7).

2. After cakes and wine, ask the Gods you worship to bless your work. Remind Them that the growth of a garden is sacred to Them.

3. Place your athame into the goblet of cider and say:

   "By my power the garden grows
   Lady's earth and Lord's sunlight,
   Through Their love the power flows
   Warmth and rain, dark and light,
   Through my magic, in fertile rows.
   So mote it be."

4. Close the circle (page 8).

5. Decant the cider into the bottle, diluting about 4 to 1 with water. Sprinkle the garden the next day, repeating your rhyme. Use the rhyme each time you sprinkle the garden with the charged cider.

Yard Gnome Magic

Yard gnomes have been around for hundreds of years. If you have one, or want one, empower it magically for luck and protection of the Earth around it.

SUPPLIES

- A yard gnome
- Incense
- Saltwater in a dish
- Your athame or wand
- A shot of whiskey (long associated with gnomes, elves, and sprites) or honey

NOTES

- Perform this spell during a waxing moon.
- Incense can include cypress, patchouli, vetivert, or vervain: All are associated with Earth as well as luck and/or protection.
- You can name your gnome and use the name in the rite, or just say "gnome."

STEPS

1. Take your gnome outside to the spot that he'll reside in.

2. Cense the gnome with incense smoke, then sprinkle with saltwater, and say:

   "By Air and Fire/Water and Earth, I consecrate this creature of protection and luck."

3. Point your athame or wand at the gnome, pouring energy through the tool, and say:

   "Awaken, creature, to your new home. [I do name you…].
   I ask you, [name], to protect this space,
   To make it your own, and bring it your blessings and your luck,
   Blessed be."

4. Raise the whiskey or honey to the gnome and say:

   "This is for you, enjoy!"

5. Bring the whiskey or honey to the gnome's mouth, then pour it on the ground at the gnome's feet.

6. Bring an offering once a month.

Land Wights and Nature Spirits

Meeting the spirits of the land where you live puts you in deeper touch with nature and yourself, and makes you and your land healthier, more fertile, and more successful.

Land wights are found in stones, trees, and tree stumps. They are protective of a space and don't like to move from it. They are often helpful but can become angry. Other nature spirits are found in plants generally, and can be more mobile and lighthearted.

Even if you live in the city, you can find land—perhaps a nature preserve, or city or state park—where you can deepen these connections, benefiting both you and the land.

SUPPLIES

- Something to leave as offering, such as:
  - Flowers or produce from your garden
  - Something sparkly (a bead, shiny coin, crystal, or stone)
  - Whiskey
  - Spring water

NOTES

- Some spirits are hostile or private—they don't want your company. If you sense this, be polite. Leave an offering and don't return.

STEPS

1. Slowly and quietly walk through an area, just being observant, noticing plants, trees, stones, and birdsong. Get to know the space.

2. Find a tree or large stone to sit by. Still your thoughts. Gently reach out with your mind to hear what this being has to say. Spend as much time as you like.

3. Leave an offering when you go.

4. If the spot welcomes you, return regularly. Learn what this spot is like at different seasons, and at various times of day.

5. Spend at least a year working with a single spot, so that you know it through a cycle of seasons.

Endnote

Continued from page 88.

We can find the solution to our negativity in our own positivity, and we can find our own positive traits within our negative self-talk. For every negative trait you have, a positive one is a part of it. Here is a sample list:

Negative	Positive
Blunt	Honest
Promiscuous	Sensual
Prudish	Selective
Messy	Relaxed about my environment
Vain	Attentive to beauty

Each negative item has a positive side. For any negative trait you have, you can find, and celebrate, its inherent good side.

In Conclusion

One of the things we learn in Wicca is to flow with cycles. Nothing is ever really over. We come to the North only to return to the East; we come to Winter only to return to Spring.

So this book isn't really over, either, and neither is your journey.

If, in these pages, working these spells and performing these rituals, you've found healing, empowerment, peace, and strength, that's a good sign that you're on the right path. Continue with it, repeating your rituals and gaining skill with experience, meditating regularly and gaining insight and serenity. Continue to draw on spellwork to protect, enhance, attract, and acknowledge; it will continue to reward you.

And, of course, continue your studies.

The resources section that follows lists a few books and online sources that will help you take the next steps. Those, too, provide additional resources, drawing you like the Pied Piper to who-knows-where. The adventure continues. I wish you many blessings.

Resources

The Elements of Ritual: Air, Fire, Water & Earth in the Wiccan Circle, by Deborah Lipp (Llewellyn Publications, 2003)

A detailed, step-by-step analysis of the Wiccan circle, with a deep dive into how and why each step is performed.

The Encyclopedia of Goddesses and Heroines, by Patricia Monaghan (New World Library, 2014)

This thoroughly researched volume is a wonderful resource, and can be used in "Finding a Personal God or Goddess" (page 14).

Have You Been Hexed? Recognizing and Breaking Curses, by Alexandra Chauran (Llewellyn Publications, 2013)

If the subject of "How to Remove a Curse" (page 122) interests you, this is my favorite book on the subject: practical, helpful, and unencumbered by the nonsense that often accompanies this subject.

Magical Power for Beginners: How to Raise & Send Energy for Spells That Work, by Deborah Lipp (Llewellyn Publications, 2017)

A detailed exploration of the "how to" of magic: performing spells, raising power, choosing a target, and designing your own spells.

The Witch's Shield: Protection Magick and Psychic Self-Defense, by Christopher Penczak (Llewellyn Publications, 2004)

In chapter 7 I talked about psychic shielding as one of the essential techniques of witchcraft. Here's a whole book on the subject by a wonderful and respected author.

Thorn Mooney's YouTube channel: YouTube.com/drawingKenaz

Thorn Mooney, author of *Traditional Wicca* (Lewellyn Publications, 2018) is *the* YouTube resource for solid, reliable information on traditionally oriented Wicca.

Music Resources (for chants and accompaniment during rituals)

Anam Cara's YouTube channel: YouTube.com/sazell33

This wide-ranging channel includes Pagan and meditation music.

Gleewood Pagan Music Examples: Gleewood.org/seeking/doing/pagan-music-examples

This list of lyric sites, music channels, and music for purchase is diverse and lovely.

Reclaiming and Starhawk's Chants MegaMix:
YouTube.com/playlist?list=PLj2mapKdxl7Ty2ePzA52JWEtUwyGGHqqh

This playlist is an invaluable resource for Pagan chants to use during spells.

References

The following resources are my constant companions when working on spells.

This text is a classic, originally published in 1909:

Crowley, Aleister, and Israel Regardie. *777 And Other Qabalistic Writings of Aleister Crowley.* York Beach, ME: Samuel Weiser, 1977.

These books have everything you need to find the correct herb or crystal for the working at hand:

Cunningham, Scott. *Cunningham's Encyclopedia of Crystal, Gem & Metal Magic.* Woodbury, MN: Llewellyn Publications, 2012.

Cunningham, Scott. *Cunningham's Encyclopedia of Magical Herbs.* Woodbury, MN: Llewellyn Publications, 2016.

To figure out exactly when to do a spell:

Astrology.com. "Planetary Hours Calculator." Accessed March 9, 2020. Astrology.com.tr /planetary-hours.asp.

For more information on land wights and nature spirits (page 176):

Khan, Molly. "Spirits of the Land: Landvaettir, Wights, and Elves." Patheos.com. July 15, 2015. Patheos.com/blogs/heathenatheart/2015/07/spirits-of-the-land-landvaettir-wights -and-elves.

Glossary

Amulet
A magical object used for protective purposes or to ward off evil. It is the opposite of a *talisman*.

Athame
A magical knife. Traditionally, it is black-handled and has a doubled-edged blade. It is used to direct energy, and most traditions say it is never for physically cutting. (See *white-handled knife*.) Some traditions add engravings to the blade or handle. It usually represents Air (in some traditions, Fire). A sword or athame is one of the four primary tools of Wicca.

Aura
An energy field that surrounds the body, extending about 2 to 3 feet.

Bind rune
A type of *sigil* combining two or three elements, usually of the Futhark alphabet (runes).

Blessed be
Used as a greeting or farewell: End an invocation with it, because you are greeting the entity invoked.

Boleen
See *white-handled knife*.

Charm
A charm can be another word for a *spell*, and like a spell, it can mean the "spelled-out" part of the magic—the words used. It can also be a magical object: an *amulet* or *talisman*.

Contagion
In magic, contagion is conveying power by having something touch something else. One drop of magical contagion spreads to the whole thing—so you could consecrate a glass of wine and the whole bottle is considered consecrated.

Coven
A group of witches who practice together. Traditional Wicca uses *coven* only for groups of initiates, and "grove" or "circle" for a more casual group.

Cup
In Wicca, this is a goblet, usually silver, pewter, or ceramic. It is used to hold ritual wine or other beverages, and represents Water. A cup is one of the four primary tools of Wicca.

Deosil

Clockwise (literally "sunwise"). Some Wiccans in the Southern Hemisphere move counter-clockwise, which is sunwise there.

Esbat

A Wiccan lunar circle. Considered a "working" circle, where magic is done.

Etheric body

The part of your *aura* that closely hugs your physical body, and holds your emotions and attachments.

Labyrinth

Generally, the difference between a labyrinth and a maze is that a maze is a puzzle, with multiple paths that dead-end, and only one correct path. A labyrinth has exactly one path, which leads to the center, and that same path leads back out. The oldest known labyrinth was found in Knossos, Crete, and dates to the Bronze Age.

Magic

Performing an act in order to cause specific desired change through non-ordinary (occult or spiritual) means.

Mojo bag

A bag containing a variety of magical ingredients that can work as an *amulet* or *talisman*.

Mundane

This word is used in the Pagan and Wiccan communities to distinguish things that are ordinary, day-to-day, and not magical, such as your *mundane* name or your *mundane* job.

Patron deity

A deity with whom you have a deep personal relationship. "Patron" can refer to a God or Goddess, even though the word's root is male: Most people don't refer to "matron deities."

Pentacle

A magical tool that is a disk with a pentagram (five-pointed star) engraved or inscribed on it. It is used as a plate and to represent Earth. A pentacle is one of the four primary tools of Wicca.

Poppet

A magical doll used to represent a person or animal.

Rite/ritual

A religious ceremony, or series of prescribed steps for a religious purpose.

Sabbat
A Wiccan solar holiday. Considered a celebratory circle where magic isn't usually done.

Sigil
Any magical symbol created for the purpose of containing energy. A *bind rune* is a specific type of sigil.

Skyclad
Nude (wearing only the sky).

"So mote it be"
A typical Pagan way to say "So be it." This phrase is used at the end of a spell or a piece of magic work to state that it is done, or demand that it be done.

Spell
At one time, *spell* referred only to the words—the "spelled out" part—of magic, and a magical act that was wordless was not called a spell. Today, it generally means any act of *magic*.

Talisman
A magical object used to bring some kind of blessing, power, or other positive quality (as opposed to an *amulet*, which protects against negative qualities).

Wand
Made of wood, and traditionally the length of the forearm, a wand is used to invoke and usually represents Fire (in some traditions, Air). It is one of the four primary tools of Wicca.

Waning
A waning moon decreases in size, and is measured from the end of the full moon to the beginning of the new moon.

Waxing
A waxing moon increases in size, and is measured from the end of the new moon to the beginning of the full moon.

White-handled knife
In Wiccan traditions that don't allow the *athame* to be used for cutting, there is often a second blade for that purpose. It is called a *white-handled knife* or a *boleen*. It has a white handle and a single edge.

Widdershins
Literally "anti-sunwise," this means to move counterclockwise. Some Wiccans in the Southern Hemisphere move clockwise.

Index

Acknowledgments

I must always acknowledge my first teacher, Susan Carberry, who taught me nearly everything, and Isaac Bonewits, who taught me everything Susan left out.

Some specific spells had particular influences:

The Baby Blessing is based on a rite by my best friend Barbara wrote for my kid, Arthur Lipp-Bonewits, after they were born. (Naturally, I have to acknowledge Arthur as well. Arthur just turned 30 as I write!)

For the Trunk Party, I was inspired by my sister Sunny and her marvelous eldest son, Curtis.

Many years ago, Ed Fitch wrote a marriage blessing that is still used by Wiccans and Pagans. Although I didn't copy a single word of it, I cannot help but have been inspired by it.

Last but most certainly not least, Susan Carberry taught me a variation on the Lighthouse Spell.

About the Author

Deborah Lipp is the author of nine books, including *Magical Power for Beginners, Tarot Interactions, The Study of Witchcraft, The Elements of Ritual, The Way of Four, The Way of Four Spellbook, Merry Meet Again,* and *The Ultimate James Bond Fan Book.* (One of these things is not like the others.)

Deborah has been teaching Wicca, magic, and the occult for over 30 years. She became a Witch and High Priestess in the 1980s, as an initiate of the Gardnerian tradition of Wicca. She's been published in *new Witch, The Llewellyn Magical Almanac, Pangaia,* and *Green Egg,* and has lectured on Pagan and occult topics on three continents.

As an active "out of the closet" member of the Pagan community, Deborah has appeared in various media discussing Wicca, including Coast to Coast AM, an A&E documentary (*Ancient Mysteries: Witchcraft in America*), television talk shows, and the *New York Times.*

In "real life," Deborah is a senior business analyst. She lives with her spouse, Melissa, and an assortment of cats, in Jersey City, New Jersey, three blocks from a really great view of the Freedom Tower. Deborah reads and teaches Tarot, obsesses over the Oscars, watches old movies, hand-paints furniture, and dabbles in numerous handcrafts.

Twitter: @DebLippAuthor
Instagram: @DebLippAuthor